Survival
Sewing

Survival Sewing

EMERGENCY FIXES FOR THE RIPS, SNAGS & TEARS OF EVERYDAY LIFE

Valerie Van Arsdale Shrader
+ Nathalie Mornu

LARK BOOKS

A Division of Sterling Publishing Co., Inc.
New York / London

Art Director:
Kristi Pfeffer

Cover Designer:
Cindy LaBreacht

**Associate
Art Director:**
Shannon Yokeley

**Art Production
Assistant:**
Jeff Hamilton

**Editorial
Assistance:**
Mark Bloom,
Cassie Moore

Illustrator:
J'aime Allene

Library of Congress Cataloging-in-Publication Data

Shrader, Valerie Van Arsdale.
  Survival sewing : emergency fixes for the rips, snags & tears of everyday
life / Valerie Van Arsdale Shrader & Nathalie Mornu. -- 1st ed.
    p. cm.
  Includes index.
  ISBN-13: 978-1-60059-122-8 (hc-plc concealed spiral : alk. paper)
  ISBN-10: 1-60059-122-1 (hc-plc concealed spiral : alk. paper)
  1. Clothing and dress--Repairing. I. Mornu, Nathalie. II. Title.
  TT720.S46 2007
  646'.6--dc22

                                    2007017193

10 9 8 7 6 5 4 3 2 1

First Edition

Published by Lark Books, A Division of
Sterling Publishing Co., Inc.
387 Park Avenue South, New York, N.Y. 10016

Text © 2007, Lark Books
Illustrations © 2007, Lark Books

Distributed in Canada by Sterling Publishing,
c/o Canadian Manda Group, 165 Dufferin Street
Toronto, Ontario, Canada M6K 3H6

Distributed in the United Kingdom by GMC Distribution Services,
Castle Place, 166 High Street, Lewes, East Sussex, England BN7 1XU

Distributed in Australia by Capricorn Link (Australia) Pty Ltd.,
P.O. Box 704, Windsor, NSW 2756 Australia

If you have questions or comments about this book, please contact:
Lark Books, 67 Broadway, Asheville, NC 28801
(828) 253-0467

Manufactured in China

ISBN 13: 978-1-60059-122-8
ISBN 10: 1-60059-122-1

For information about custom editions, special sales, premium and
corporate purchases, please contact Sterling Special Sales Department
at 800-805-5489 or specialsales@sterlingpub.com.

Table of Contents

STITCH HAPPENS

Is that the sound of despair you just heard?

Maybe, if the rip was the hem of your cutest skirt caught in your cutest heels while the cutest guy you've ever seen is waiting at the door. Or if the pop is a seam gone wild on your way to a meeting with the boss. Or if the boing is a wayward button bouncing off your shirt, glancing off the sink, and landing in the toilet bowl with a sinister *plop!* while a taxi is honking outside. Oh, the horror.

Life is full of such emergencies. But a little knowledge and a bit of sewing skill will help you survive whatever life throws at you (or cruelly rips from you, as the case may be). This emergency manual will give you the goods on responding to dire clothing disasters, and we'll also share some fixes for less urgent problems—need to hem a great pair of sale pants, anyone? We also offer strategies for some handy repairs around su casa—energetic puppy or mischievous cat, anybody?

Don't know the business end of the needle from a Swiss army knife? Not to worry. We start with the most basic skill ever—threading a needle—and offer you easy fixes for the problems we discuss inside. And guess what? Right here in *Survival Sewing* you'll also find the essential stuff you need to fix simple emergencies, things like a little thread, a few buttons, some needles, and other assorted supplies. (Are we thoughtful or what?) You'll also find out how to navigate the uncharted waters of a fabric shop to re-supply when the stuff in our handy little kit has been used up. We'll give you some ways to use alternate tools in a pinch—you'd be surprised what you can fix with a stapler. And, just because we are *so* thoughtful, we've also included some 30-Second Fixes for desperate moments, as well as some Exit Strategies in the face of imminent disaster.

Every man, woman, and child needs these vital skills to survive in the urban jungle. Stitch happens. Be prepared.

Emergency
PREPAREDNESS

When sewing to survive humiliating rips and tears, it helps to have the proper supplies. But wait—don't reach for the kit yet! Let's perform some reconnaissance first.

(Anatomy of a) Needle

Your primary weapon is the needle. It has two important features—an eye, which holds the thread, and a point, which spears the cloth. The needle pulls the thread through the fabric, and thus it sews. Simple, huh?

Now, here's a quiz to see if you're paying attention.

Which end is the sharp end?

    A. The point
    B. The eye
    C. All of the above

A is the correct answer!

Keep a packet of all-purpose needles on hand for sewing emergencies. The packet holds assorted lengths, with eyes of different sizes. One specialty needle that you may find useful is the embroidery needle; we suggest you add easy embroidery to your arsenal of survival skills, too. You'll see why later on.

Thread

If a needle is your weapon, thread is your ammunition.

For the trauma-induced sewing in this book, select multipurpose polyester sewing thread. It's strong and durable, yet versatile enough to use on anything from apparel to slipcovers. If you need to repair a heavy fabric that will get lots of wear and tear, use a heavy-duty thread, such as the kind sold for upholstery.

Ideally, you'd use a thread identical in color to the item you're fixing, but in an emergency, make do with whatever's on hand. If you don't have the right color, use thread that's a shade darker than the fabric. And if you can't get any kind of match, go with gray.

If you're not in full-blown disaster mode, embroidery floss may also be an ally. You can use very basic stitches to add some panache to your patches, as well as disguise things like little stains and holes.

Needle Threader

If you can't see very well up close, or if you're coordination-challenged, a needle threader will help you get the thread through the eye of the needle.

Scissors

Desperate times require desperate measures. You'll need some type of cutting tool when you're confronting disaster. Your dentist will not want you to use your teeth.

The most versatile tool for emergency sewing is a pair of embroidery scissors. They're short, which does create more work when cutting long pieces of fabric, but the small size also keeps them portable.

You want the blades to stay as sharp as possible, so don't dull them by using them to cut paper. And don't *ever* use crummy scissors like the ones they gave you in grade school. They're rarely sharp enough to cut thread, much less fabric. They're worse than using your teeth!

(On) Pins (and Needles)

Pins fasten layers of fabric together temporarily so things stay in place while you sew. Just like needles, pins have a sharp point; that's the business end. The party end sometimes has a colorful plastic ball clearly identifying it as the playful side; this is called a ballpoint pin (not to be confused with a ballpoint pen, which is completely useless for holding fabric together). You'll also see dressmaker pins that have just a flat little nub instead of a ball.

To keep from getting poked, it's a good idea to store pins in a little box (they're sold in one, so it's a no-brainer) or jabbed into a pincushion.

Safety Pins

Safety pins can do all kinds of things in a pinch: keep a waistband closed, prevent a shirt from gaping open, pick out a seam, mark a hemline. If you're the type who sees them as a form of body jewelry, we suggest you keep the ones for adornment separate from the ones for sewing. Just an idea.

Hooks + Eyes

Just like PB&J, a hook and an eye belong together. Hooks can be accompanied by either a loop eye or a straight eye. Or, you can buy a bar hook and eye. The type of eye you'll use depends on where they're placed on your garment. You'll learn more about that on page 82.

Button Up!

Buttons are such a major component in keeping our clothes on, it's hard to believe they only came into common use some 150 years ago. Before the Industrial Revolution, they were bling only the wealthy could afford.

Nowadays, they're so cheap new garments frequently come with a spare button in a little baggie that's attached to the price tag. Save those buttons! It's easy—really. If you're not the orderly type, just make it a habit to always toss the spares in the same junk drawer. And if you do things in a more systematic fashion (so much the better for confronting disasters), you can store them in a shoebox or something.

Manufacturers must be catching on to the fact that most of us are disorganized, because they frequently attach an extra button somewhere inside the clothing. What a deal—a spare part that travels with the garment! Even if your clothes don't have an extra button hiding somewhere, in an emergency, you can ask a friend to go someplace private, lock the door, and check to see if theirs do.

 *Snaps*

Snaps are extra fasteners to keep the edges of garments flat, but they don't have much load-bearing capacity, so don't expect them to resist strain if you've gained a few pounds. (For that type of emergency, you'll have to find a weight-loss book.)

You'll generally see metal snaps, although they come in plastic, too. They range from teeny to heavy-duty. If you're uncertain what size to use, go with something smaller rather than larger.

 *Fusible Web + So On*

For the sewing impaired, a fusible product is a dream come true. You don't need thread, you don't use a needle; in fact, you don't sew at all!

Loosely explained, fusible web is a network of fibers that melt when heated. You put fusible web between two layers of fabric, run a hot iron over the cloth, and—presto!—the layers are glued together. You can buy it by the yard (as for appliqué), or get a narrow strip on a spool, which is ideal for hems or similar skinny emergencies. There are two types of fusible web—one has a paper backing, and the other doesn't. Another handy product is fabric glue, an adhesive formulated especially for bonding cloth.

Nothing's perfect, of course. Fusible web doesn't work on all fabrics because of the level of heat that must be used. Even worse, fusible web opens up all kinds of possibilities for disaster if you're not careful. If it's not positioned properly between two layers of fabric, you could bond your shirt to the iron! Treat fusible web like heavy machinery—don't use it while under the influence.

Seam (the) Ripper

A seam ripper vaguely resembles a harpoon. Don't let its appearance fool you—it's an immensely helpful thing. It's also *very* sharp.

While you would use it to open up seams, a seam ripper also serves to take apart hems when you want to make pants or skirts longer. It's indispensable for removing those itchy labels that drive you crazy, as well as the annoying ones that stick up out of your collar. (In a pinch, it could probably spear olives for a martini, too.)

in the kit Measuring Devices

Real seamstresses use a tape measure for the tasks that require precision from the get-go, such as altering a hem or moving a button. You'll need some kind of measuring device for these maneuvers, too.

When engaged in true survival sewing, you need to be quick on your feet. If there's no tape measure in sight, you can use a ruler, a piece of paper with marks on it, or even a bit of string cut to the right length to complete an impromptu measuring task.

Iron

To the novice, an iron is just an appliance that gets wrinkles out of clothes. The survival sewer, however, is no fool, and recognizes it as a versatile tool. To avoid bombarding you with information now, we'll tell you all about this later.

The best irons have a high-quality, non-stick ironing surface. They have a wide temperature range to accommodate all kinds of fabrics, and have a steam feature that makes short work of all pressing tasks.

Patches + Trim

Sometimes (often, actually), the easiest way to fix a hole or a rip or a tear is to simply cover it up with a patch. For those down in the trenches who need a quick-and-dirty fix, a plain commercial iron-on patch is the bomb; just follow the instructions on the package to confront the calamity.

Although these patches certainly work, they aren't actually beautiful. While you can buy decorative patches, you can also make your own patches from fabric if you're feeling clever and artistic. You could even go so far as to call one of these fancy patches an *appliqué*, if you'd like. When we Get Your Fix On, we'll teach you how to attach a decorative patch as well as make your own cool patch (page 32).

Trim, such as ribbon, rickrack, or bobbles, can also be used to cover up little uh-ohs. Think of it as a lovely bandage.

GETTING
Your Fix On

You've completed the first part of your training. Now we introduce the skills that will make you a true sewing survivor. Be advised that you may be asked to simulate emergency conditions in this chapter. In other words, get ready to perform some practice drills.

Threading a Needle

Before you address any sewing emergency, you must first master the needle and thread. This is an important skill in your arsenal, so get focused. Ready?

1 Snip about 15 inches (38.1 cm) of thread. Place the scissors at about a 45° angle to the thread, so you make a slanted cut in the thread (figure 1).

2 This is important: Dampen one end of the thread by pulling its tip between your puckered lips; this will pull all the fibers together and face them in the same direction.

3 Now, this is also important: screw one of your eyes tightly shut so you don't see double, and, while squinting at the eye of the needle, gently run the damp end of the thread through it (figure 2). Sticking out your tongue may help you aim better. Some find that scrunching up the nose is equally effective.

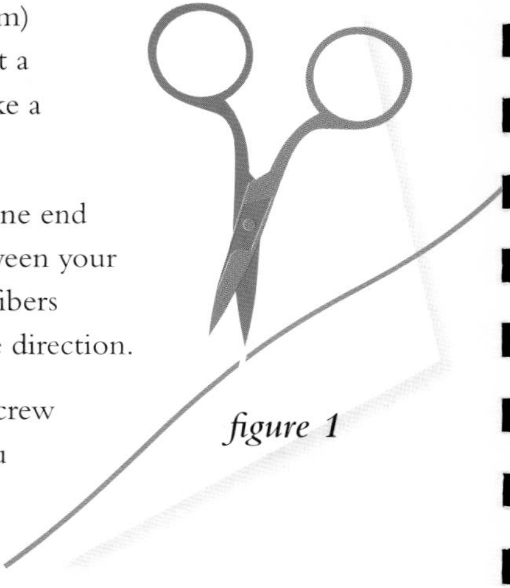

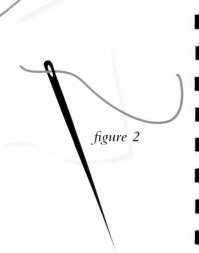

figure 1

figure 2

Using a Needle Threader

If eyesight or coordination fail you at a critical juncture, you can always use a needle threader. Of course, we consider that cheating, but we'll let you make the call on that.

1 Slip the thin wire of the needle threader through the eye of the needle. Slide the thread through the wire (figure 3).

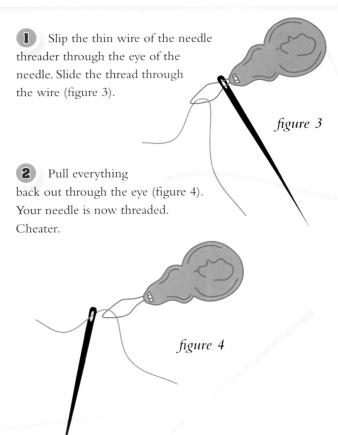

figure 3

2 Pull everything back out through the eye (figure 4). Your needle is now threaded. Cheater.

figure 4

Tying the Knot

Okay, so you've successfully guided one end of the thread through the eye of the needle. Congrats—the toughest part's over! Now, to knot a single strand of thread so the end won't pull out, we give you two different methods. Try one, and if it works for you, you can ignore the other. Or else try both, then stick with whichever one you think's easier. Learn how to knot a double strand on page 22.

Note: These directions are for the right-handed. If you're a southpaw, reverse them.

Method Number One

1 About an inch (2.5 cm) from the end, create a loop of thread and pinch it between your thumb and index finger. Make certain that the thread leading to the needle is in front of the end, as shown in figure 5.

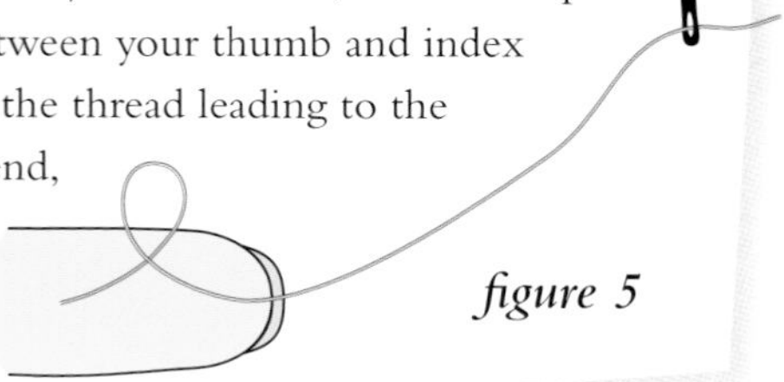

figure 5

2 Bring the needle through the loop from behind (see figure 6) and pull 'til the knot tightens. Voilà! If your knot should happen to pull through the fabric when you tackle your emergency, repeat this delicate procedure a second time to make the knot bigger.

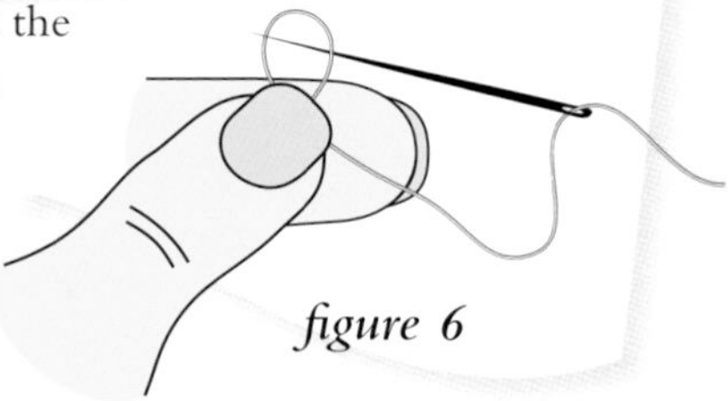

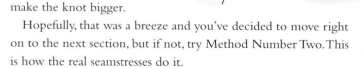

figure 6

Hopefully, that was a breeze and you've decided to move right on to the next section, but if not, try Method Number Two. This is how the real seamstresses do it.

Method Number Two

1 Holding the needle in the right hand, wrap the end of the thread once around your left index finger, as shown in figure 7. Use your thumb to roll the wrap down the index finger just a wee bit toward the knuckle (see figure 8). The idea is to slightly tangle the wrapped thread around itself.

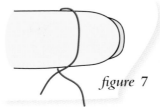

figure 7

2 Roll it back to the fingertip, snare it between the pad of the thumb and the nail of the index finger as shown in figure 9, and pull firmly with your right hand, which is still holding the needle and thread, until you get a tight little knot.

figure 8

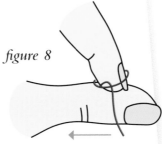

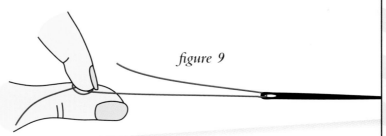

figure 9

Your first few attempts at Method Number Two may net you a big snarl, but don't be discouraged—you may just be rolling the wrap too much.

Double Strand Knot

Occasionally, you may need to use a double strand of thread to combat an emergency. Reinforcements, you know.

1 Pull the thread through the eye of the needle, with an equal amount of thread on each side.

2 Put your helmet on. Knot both ends together as in Method Number One (figure 10).

3 Just kidding about the helmet.

With all the preliminaries out of the way, it's time to jump into what we're really here to do: some survival sewing.

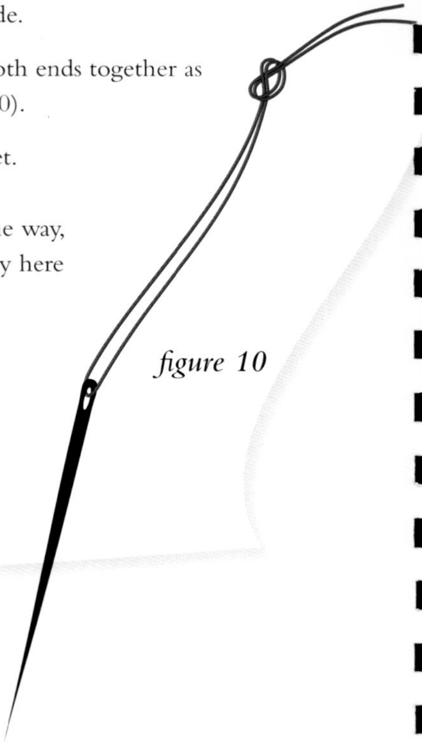

figure 10

Stitching It Up

Aren't you proud of yourself? You've conquered threading the needle and tying a knot. Now it's time to get into the trenches and learn some stitches. Once you get the hang of them, you can fix most anything. Scout's honor. Begin all of these stitches by knotting the thread and then inserting the needle into the wrong side of the fabric so the knot won't show.

Running Stitch

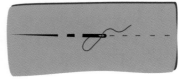

The running stitch just scoots right across the fabric. It's a very basic stitch. Simply weave the needle in and out of the fabric, keeping the size of the stitches as uniform as you can (figure 11).

figure 11

Backstitch

This is the stitch to use for repairing seams. The backstitch is perfect for these emergency situations, because it's quick and strong, and no one will notice your repair, because it mimics the look of machine-sewn stitching. The thread overlaps on one side, forming a tightly stitched line.

To backstitch, anchor the thread (this means pull the needle through the fabric until the knot catches) about ⅛ inch (3 mm) to the left of where you want the first stitch to start. Insert the needle to the right, and then back through ¼ inch (6 mm) to the left. Stick the needle back through at the end of the previous stitch (figure 12). Repeat this action until the crisis has been resolved.

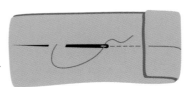

figure 12

If for some reason you're intimidated by the backstitch, you can fudge by using the running stitch, working in one direction until you've reached the end of the mishap. Then, stitch back in the opposite direction, filling in the stitches (figure 13). You'll have a complete line of stitching on each side of the fabric.

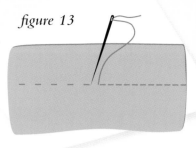

figure 13

Satin Stitch

The satin stitch is a good mending stitch, because you can use a pretty line of stitching to fix a tear, especially if you use a fun color of thread. The satin stitch is simply a row of straight stitches all snuggled up against one another (figure 14).

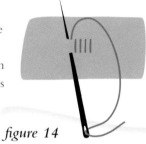

figure 14

Whipstitch

Here's another workhorse of a stitch. You can sew two edges together very tightly with this baby. Working from the wrong side, insert the needle perpendicular to the fabric edge, over and over and over again (figure 15). The stitches will be slanted.

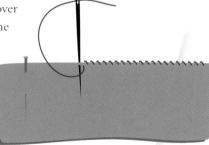

figure 15

Hem Stitch

Okay, there are fancy ways to hem, and there's this way. We're teaching this way.

With the needle inserted through the fold of the fabric, pick up just a thread or two in the garment. Now insert the needle

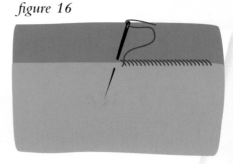

figure 16

into the fold again (figure 16). Repeat and repeat and repeat; like whipstitch, this stitch also makes slanted stitches.

Slipstitch

The slipstitch is especially good when you have to repair something that you can't turn inside out. Like a pillow with no zipper.

figure 17

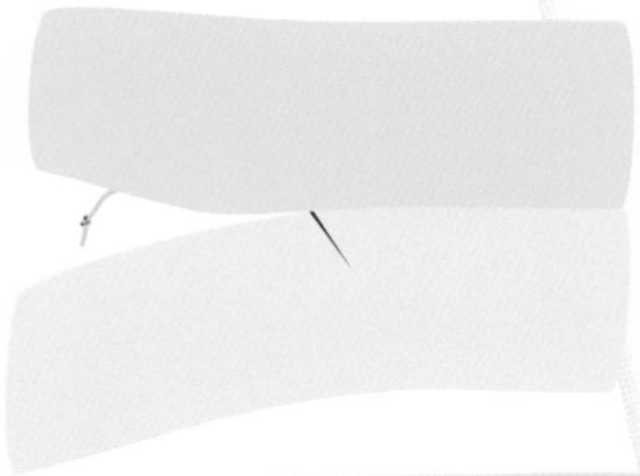

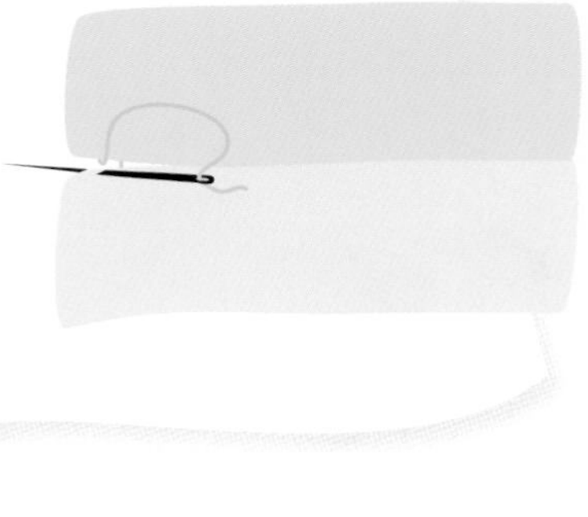

Working from the right side, slip the needle through one end of the open seam to anchor the thread (figure 17). Take a small stitch through the fold and pull the needle through. Insert the needle directly opposite the end of the stitch you just made, and take a stitch through the other fold.

It will pull the edges together lovingly. Keep on keepin' on as needed (figure 18).

Tack

A tack is just a bunch of straight stitches used to join layers of fabric together. You can repeat several of them in place for a sturdy connection (figure 19).

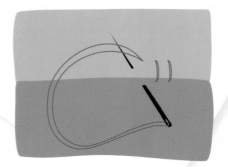

figure 19

Blindstitch

Think of blindstitch as shy. Because it remains inconspicuous on either side of the garment, it's perfect for stitching linings to clothing.

Working from right to left, make a small horizontal stitch that picks up just a thread of lining fabric; ¼ inch (6 mm) to the left, pick up a thread in the garment. Repeat, alternating between fabrics (figure 20).

figure 20

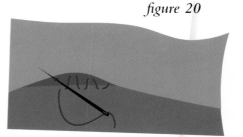

Ending the Stitching

Since your training has gone so well, perhaps you're wondering how to stop sewing. Now that you've got the hang of stitching, this part is a breeze.

Using a Backstitch

You have a couple of options. The first is simply to make a few backstitches at the end of your line of stitching. If you don't remember how to do that, no big deal: just refer to page 23.

Making a Knot

The other choice is to knot the thread. It's easy as 1, 2, 3! To make a knot, work on the wrong side of the fabric.

figure 21

1 As you make the last stitch, don't pull it completely tight, but leave a small loop, as shown in figure 21.

2 Pull the needle through the loop until you form another small loop (see figure 22).

figure 22

3 Finally, insert the needle through the second loop (see figure 23) and pull the thread tight to form a small knot. That's all there is to it!

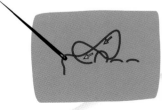

figure 23

Wielding a Seam Ripper

In survival sewing, you may want to take out stitching to alter a hem or remove unnecessary threads. The seam ripper's the right tool for these jobs.

The sharp blade of the seam ripper is in the curved area near the point. This is the part that does the ripping. Use this tool cautiously, because it's all too easy to poke another hole while you're desperately trying to make a repair.

1 Let's start with an easy one: say your button popped off, but a big blob of thread remains in the fabric. Carefully insert the tip of the seam ripper under all the threads and gently lift them out (figure 24). If some refuse to cooperate, you can gently cut them with the tool's blade.

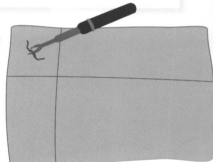

figure 24

2 To rip out a straight-stitched seam, place the garment down with the seam closed, slip the point of the seam ripper under every fifth stitch, and cut (figure 25). Turn the garment over and pick out the threads on the other side.

figure 25

3 If you want to change a hemline, you'll need to remove the original stitching. Some hems may be straight stitched as described above; pick them out using the same procedure. Some hems have two lines of stitching and you may have to rip out both, by the way.

4 Now, to complicate matters slightly, many commercial garments have the edges stitched together on a fancy machine called a *serger*. For hems where you see serging, don't be in a big rush to remove it all. Most likely, the garment was first serged to prevent the fabric from fraying, and then a special, practically invisible hemstitch was made by another fancy machine. If you pull the hem away from the garment, you can see these stitches. Just push the seam ripper under the hem to cut a stitch as done in figure 26, pull a little to expose the next stitch, then cut it.

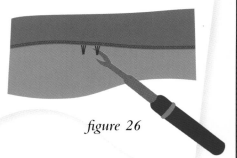

figure 26

After the emergency maneuvers have been completed, use tweezers or masking tape to remove the stray threads. Press and steam the fabric gently after taking out the stitches. This will help close needle holes and restore the weave of the fabric.

Using Your Iron

Of course, out there in the urban jungle, you're not going to be packing an iron. But for lesser emergencies that can be confronted at home, an iron is a handy tool.

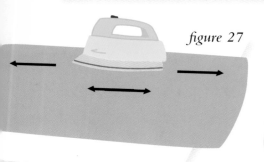

figure 27

figure 28

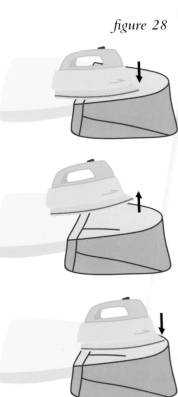

There's a big difference between *ironing* and *pressing*. Ironing is sliding the iron across the expanse of fabric (figure 27). When we use an iron to help resolve crises in this book, we're usually going to be *pressing*. Pressing is moving the iron across the fabric by pressing it down, picking it straight up, moving to another area, and pressing down again (figure 28). No sliding allowed!

Adding Patches + Appliqués

If you're feeling a little holey-than-thou, here's the survival skill for you. For holes or burns (or even tears), the best fix is usually a patch.

Adding a Commercial Patch

1 If you're not particular, you could slap on an iron-on patch, following the manufacturer's instructions (figure 29).

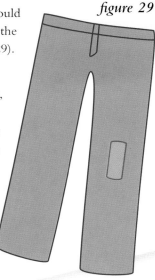

figure 29

2 You can also use commercial patches of any type (you know, stars, roses, kitschy little things like that), some of which are iron-on, too. For those that aren't, just pin your patch in place over the hole and sew on with the stitch of your choice. (Hint: the backstitch is the most secure, so we used it in figure 30.)

figure 30

Making Your Own Patch

While a commercial patch is the quick-and-dirty fix, it's easy to make your own patches, too.

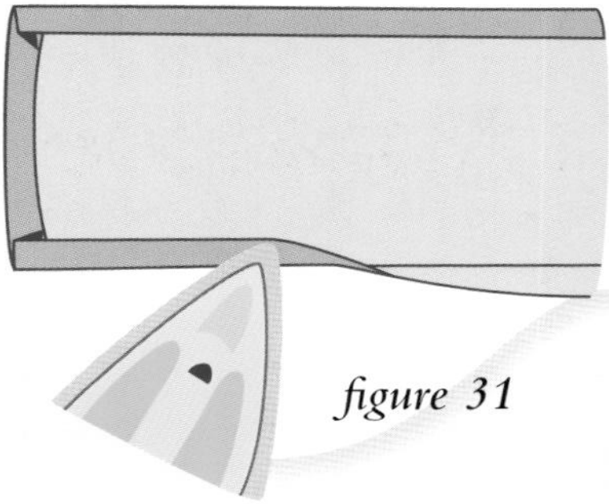

1 Take a piece of fabric, press the raw edges under (figure 31), and stitch it in place over your boo-boo. (Scared to shop for fabric? Calm down. We'll teach you how on page 107.) You can also use fusible web to secure the raw edges when you press them under.

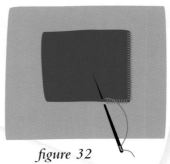

figure 31

2 There are some variations on this idea, of course. If you're the edgy, deconstructed type, don't even worry about turning under the edges before you stitch the patch down. Encasing the edges with a satin stitch is a good idea, though (figure 32).

figure 32

3 If you're still the edgy, deconstructed type, you can also use pinking shears to cut out a patch and then stitch it on with a simple running stitch (figure 33).

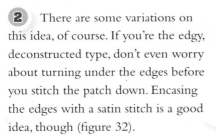

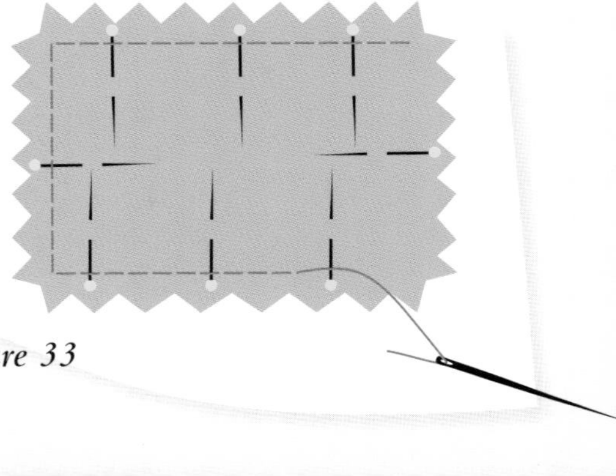

figure 33

Making Your Own Iron-On Patch

Suppose you become truly inspired by this make-your-own patch idea? You can make your own custom iron-on patches using that miraculous paper-backed fusible web stuff.

1 Begin by tracing (or drawing) your chosen pattern onto the paper backing of the fusible web. (Your patch will be the reverse of the pattern you draw, be forewarned.) Cut out the traced pattern roughly, leaving a margin around the design.

2 Press the tracing, fusible side down, onto the wrong side of the fabric to fuse. Cut out the patch on the traced outline (figure 34).

figure 34

3 Now, peel off the paper backing and fuse the patch over the hole (figure 35). Just to be on the safe side, be sure to follow the manufacturer's instructions for fusing the specific brand of web you end up with.

figure 35

It's time for another quiz.

What is appliqué?

    A. A French pastry

    B. A fancy new cell phone

    C. I don't know, because you haven't told me yet

C is the correct answer!

A patch is a thing that repairs a hole, while an appliqué is a decorative piece of fabric that is applied to a surface. Thus, you can probably see that an appliqué can also be a patch, just a lovelier one.

Using Pizzazz When You Mend

Fortunately, not all clothing disasters have to be dealt with immediately. If you've got a little time, your repair can also be a work of art. You can use decorative trim, patches, and stitching to disguise (ahem!) flaws.

Using Ribbon

Ribbon can be added with the hand stitch of your choice to cover up anything that needs to be covered up, be it a mended tear (more about this on page 48) or a little hole or a tiny stain. Trims come in many widths, which is perfect for the accidents of various magnitudes that may befall your stuff. If the fiber content of the ribbon and the repairee allow, you can also use fusible web to attach the ribbon.

1 If you're attaching wide ribbon, you'll probably want to use a row of stitching at each edge to secure the ribbon (figure 36).

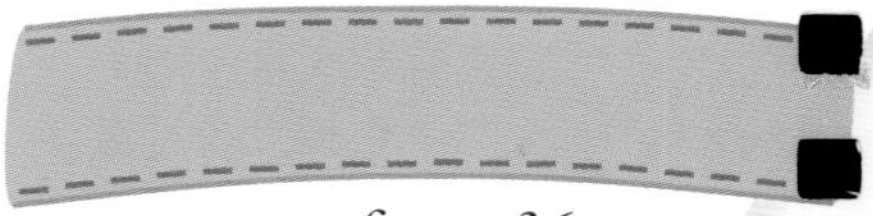

figure 36

2 Narrow ribbon is less demanding and can be applied with only one row of stitching (figure 37).

figure 37

3 Funky little trims like bobbles or pompoms should be stitched on along the band (figure 38).

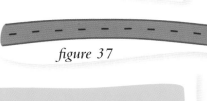

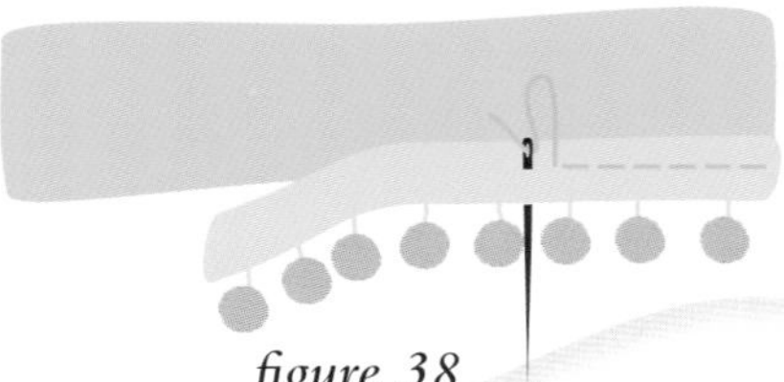

figure 38

While lace is lovely, remember that it is sheer and may not disguise what's under it quite as well as an opaque trim might. On the flip side, it's very easy to disguise your stitching when you're working with lace.

Adding Embroidery

figure 39

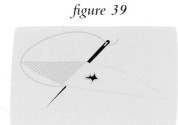

Some simple (and we do mean *simple*) embroidery can be enlisted to help survive a mishap. Remember the satin stitch? Well, it can be used to create all sorts of motifs for creative mending. (The design in figure 39 looks a bit like a leaf, doesn't it?) Because it's thicker than thread, floss is higher on the eye-candy meter.

1 Embroidery floss has several *plies* (strands) and it's most successfully used when you separate the plies and work with two or three strands at a time (figure 40). So begin by doing this. Of course, you'll need to use that special embroidery needle (with a large eye) to thread the multiple plies.

figure 40

2 In real-life embroidery, knots are frowned upon and the floss is secured by some tricky stitching maneuvers. But in gonzo embroidery (that's the kind we're advocating here), knots are okay. Simply place a knot in the end of your embroidery floss just as you would regular thread and have at it.

Although trim and embroidery can cover small stuff, sometimes the area you need to, ah, *repurpose* is big. Remember that a large-scale disaster is best covered with a patch. Or two.

WHEN *Disaster* Strikes YOUR CLOTHES

Now we'll take our skills into the field
as we examine real-life situations requiring
a cool head and a threaded needle.
Do not attempt to re-create these crises
at home. Eventually, they'll happen to
you anyway. Be prepared!

Repairing a Ripped Seam

This may be the most common emergency sewing situation. You can be assured that this catastrophe won't happen in the privacy of your apartment. Instead, you'll be on public display, with your seams (and perhaps more embarrassing stuff) hanging out.

1 Take a deep breath and reach for your survival sewing kit. Run, don't walk, to the nearest private place and remove the offending garment. Turn it inside out.

2 If you have straight pins or a safety pin handy, pin the seams back together after aligning the edges as best you can. Trim away the loose threads from the ripped seam.

3 Thread your needle with thread close to the original color. Use a double strand of thread if you want. Remember to knot it.

4 Use the backstitch (page 23) to repair the seam (figure 1), beginning and ending about an inch (2.5 cm) into the still-sewn part of the seam. Remember to knot the thread after you've brought the situation under control.

figure 1

30-SECOND FIX

Oh, no. Your significant other's mother is waiting to take you to lunch. You have a reservation at a stuffy restaurant. Your demonic pants have just sprung a leak in a most inappropriate spot. Grab a stapler and head to that private place. Remove the pants, align the seams, and staple them back together along the seamline. In your frenzy, remember to put the pants back on.

Sewing on a Button

Okay, so you're getting ready for work, you're already late, and a button pops off your shirt. You could pull another shirt out of your closet, but you've already spent precious time ironing the one that lost its button. Or (duh!), you could whip out a needle and thread and sew that button right back on in a flash. Sewing on a button is so easy they teach it in preschool. If four- and five-year-old kids can do it, you can too.

Two-Hole Button

1 Cut a length of thread that matches the color on your shirt, if you can. If you can't, gray or beige will do. Thread the needle, using a double strand of thread for this repair job.

2 Look for the place where that pesky button once hung— clues include bits of thread poking out of the fabric, some faint holes, or a spot that looks a bit worn. If you don't see any telltale signs, button the remaining buttons and push a pin through the center of the buttonhole to mark the spot for the button.

3 Working from the wrong side of the garment, poke the needle up through the spot where you want to reattach the button. Pull it carefully to avoid snarling the thread until the knot is set.

4 Push the needle through the back of one of the holes in the button; let it fall down the thread to rest on the fabric (figure 2). Place a pin, toothpick, or matchstick flat over the top of the buttonholes.

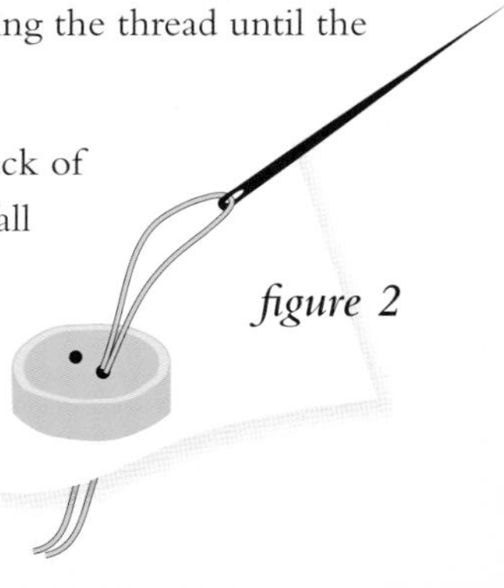

figure 2

5 Push the needle back down through the other hole and into the fabric. Pull the thread until the button is tight against the cloth. Push the needle up and down through the holes several times, sewing in the same direction (figure 3).

figure 3

6 Bring the needle up through the fabric to the right side and remove the pin, toothpick, or matchstick. To allow the button to slip through the buttonhole, create a thread shank by winding the thread under the button a few times (figure 4), then poke the needle back to the wrong side of the fabric. Make a knot and cut the thread.

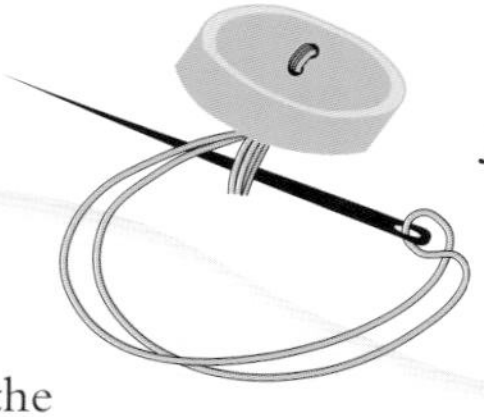

figure 4

Four-Hole Button

1 Follow the instructions for the two-hole button. Don't forget to place a pin, toothpick, or matchstick flat over the top of the buttonholes.

2 Start with the needle going from the first hole to the one next to it; after you've repeated this several times, repeat on the other pair of holes to create two lines of parallel stitching (figure 5).

The parallel lines described above look most professional, but you could also sew the thread in an X, or in a square by working from hole to hole.

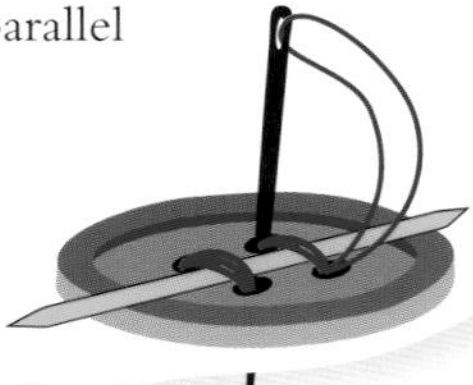

figure 5

Shank Back Button

1 Knot the thread and push the needle up from the back of the fabric. Run the needle through the shank and back down through the right side of the fabric about ¹⁄₁₆ inch (1.6 mm) from the incoming thread; make sure the shank aligns with the direction of the buttonhole.

2 Working from the wrong side, carefully pull the thread until the button is tight against the clothing. Stitch up and down around the shank several times, sewing in the same direction (figure 6). With the needle on the wrong side of the fabric, make a knot and cut the thread.

figure 6

30-SECOND FIX

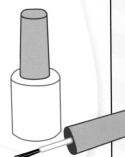

An ounce of prevention is worth a pound of humiliation. Here's a fasten-ating tip if you spot a button that's trying to escape—to prevent or stop fraying button threads, dab a little clear nail polish on the problem spot. After it dries, trim away any loose thread. When you've got more time, sew the button back on for real.

EXIT STRATEGY

Didn't you schedule a dentist's appointment for, uh, right about now? Best get going if you don't want to be late for that filling. (No one at work needs to know you're going shopping for another shirt!)

Fixing a Cuff

Not only is it tacky to have a floppy cuff on your pants, it's dangerous because your heels could get tangled in the fabric and cause a wipe-out. Here's a fix-it job that's less about saving face and more about not falling on your face!

Thanks to the tacking stitch explained on page 26, this job is a cinch.

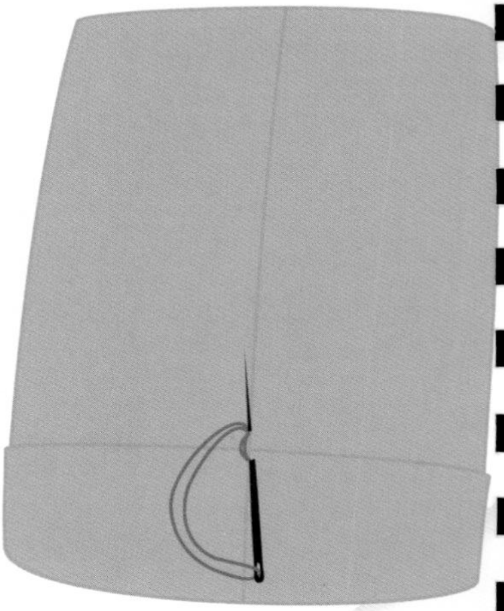

1 Use your detective skills to discover where the cuff was originally tacked down. It's usually at both the outer and inner seams of the pants. You should be able to recognize it by locating the frayed threads from the original tacking.

2 Use a double strand of thread and whip a few tacking stitches to the spot you just sniffed out with your highly developed sleuthing skills, making sure to take the thread through the cuff *and* the leg of the pants (figure 7). Maybe you might want to pin the cuff in place before you get started. Maybe not.

figure 7

30-SECOND FIX

The workday is over. Your social life depends on making the subway on time, but your loose cuff prevents you from sprinting to the stop. If you don't have a needle and thread handy, you can always safety pin the cuff (from the inside) to hold it in place 'til you access your emergency sewing kit.

Reviving a Hem

While droopy hems aren't life threatening like a wayward cuff, they do reflect poorly on your ability to maintain your wardrobe. Depending on the circumstances (remember that cute guy at the door?), this emergency could score big on the Richter scale.

Now, you have two options, depending on the location of your emergency: the no-sew fix, or the know-sew mend.

The No-Sew Fix

Although this approach gets the job done in a nanosecond, you must have access to an iron to make this repair. We're using paper-backed fusible web in the first example.

1 Plug in an iron to preheat it.

2 Measure along the unstitched part of the hemline to determine how much fusible web tape you need. Cut that length of fusible tape.

3 On the wrong side of the garment (that's the inside, the side that doesn't show), put the fusible web down on the side of the hem that will eventually fold over the garment, placing the web with the rough side against the fabric and the paper backing facing up. Use a pin or two to keep it in place if necessary.

4 Lift the iron over the fusible web and…pause. Look carefully at the fusible web: is the paper backing facing up, the way we told you to place it? Because if it's not, you're about to melt the adhesive right onto the iron. Then you'll have a mess to clean up *and* a ruined garment stuck to the iron—although that kind of solves the issue of fixing the hem, doesn't it?

Okay, with the orientation of the fusible tape safely double-checked, follow the manufacturer's instructions to press the fusible web and stick it to the clothing (figure 8).

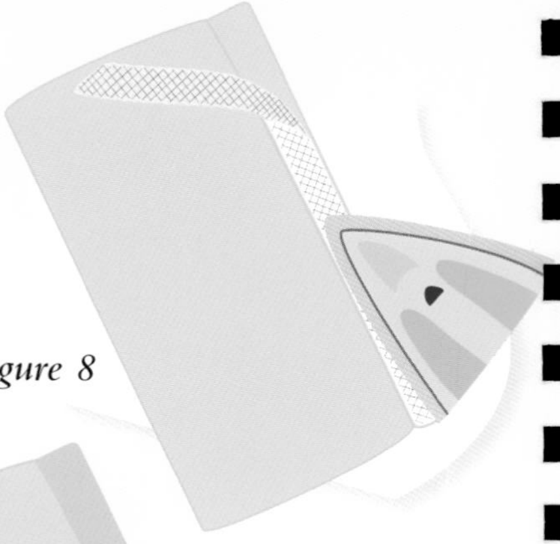

figure 8

5 Peel away the paper backing from the fusible web. Flip the hem over so that the fusible web tape is now inside the fold. Once again, press (figure 9).

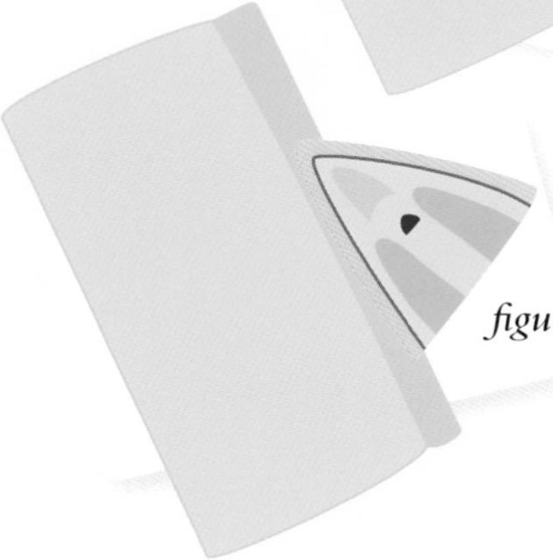

figure 9

Now let's use fusible web without a paper backing. Simply insert it between the edges you want to fuse and press (figure 10).

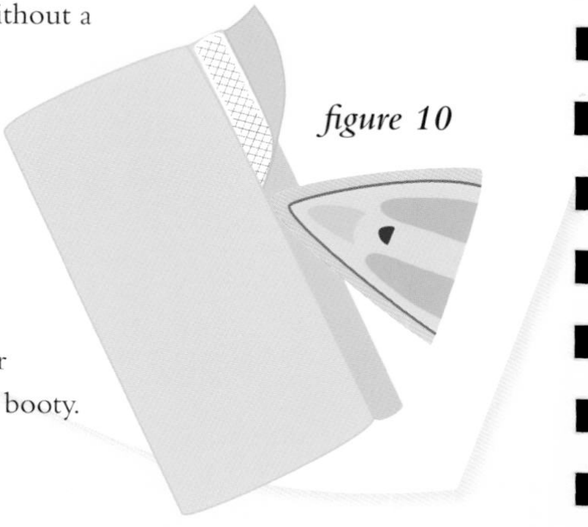

figure 10

Although fusible web tape may not survive repeated trips through the washer and dryer and adds a little stiffness to your garment, it can really save your booty.

The Know-Sew Mend

With just a needle, some thread, and a minute or two, you can permanently fix a hem. Remember that hemstitches should appear almost invisible from the outside, so take the tiniest stitches possible when sewing through the part of the fabric that shows.

1 At the spot where the hem's coming apart, you'll probably still see at least one crease line. Turn the fabric under along any creases so it no longer sags and pin it into place (figure 11).

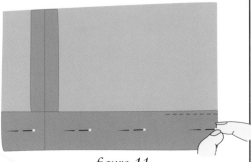

figure 11

2 Cut a piece of thread the same color as the one used for the rest of the hem (or neutral gray). You know the drill by now: thread the needle and tie a knot in the end of one strand of thread. For this stitch, you'll sew with only a single strand of thread.

3 Working from the wrong side of the garment (again, that's the side that doesn't show), insert the needle about ½ inch (1.3 cm) past where the hem has come apart. Go through the fold, but not the garment (figure 12).

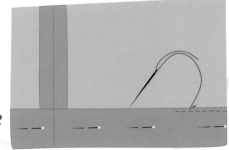

figure 12

4 Start stitching toward the other end of the gap in the hem. Need a reminder of how to hemstitch? Here are your helpful authors to the rescue:

Use the needle to pick up just a thread or two in the garment. Insert the needle back up into the fold again. Take a stitch that's a bit bigger to run the needle back through the fold and again pick up just a thread or two in the garment. Repeat (figure 13). Don't pull the stitches too tightly, or the fabric will pucker.

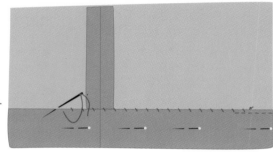

figure 13

5 Continue hemstitching 'til you get to ½ inch (1.3 cm) beyond where the original hem is still sewn together. Tie off the thread and snip it.

30-SECOND FIX

You feel a panic attack coming—you've got a speech to give and your hem is sagging, just like your spirits. Grab your tape dispenser and apply short pieces of tape along the droopy hemline. You've saved the day (and maybe your job, too). Just remember to pull off the tape before you wash the inconsiderate article of clothing.

Disguising Holes, Stains, Tears + Burns

While these kinds of problems are certainly emergencies, and can be quite serious, they often require a little more time to repair, we're sorry to say. In other words, resign yourself to the fact that an immediate solution may not be available for this vexing category of disaster, short of a quick exit. Bearing this in mind, let's view the solutions as opportunities, shall we?

Stubborn stains, holes, and burns are all mishaps that need to be covered up with something—a patch, some embroidery, an appliqué. Most of these repairs fall into our fixing-with-flair category, because sometimes these repairs happen in very visible areas. Let's examine some for-instances.

Camouflaging a Hole

During a crafting frenzy—while holding a project in your lap—you accidentally snipped a little hole in your shirt. Now what?

1 A little tiny hole (figure 14) can be turned into a blooming flower with a center of satin stitches and some la-di-da running stitches. Begin by mending the hole with satin stitches; these are on page 24, if you've forgotten how to make them.

figure 14

2 Use the running stitch (on page 23, for the forgetful) to create dainty little petals surrounding the mend (figure 15). To create a decorative effect, add as many blooming flowers as you'd like. Likewise, imagine covering up an obstinate latte splatter in the same fashion.

figure 15

Mending a Tear

Suppose you have a clean rip in a not-so-visible spot? Why, you simply mend the tear.

1 Fortify each edge of the tear with a strip of lightweight fusible interfacing (figure 16), available at your friendly neighborhood fabric store. Follow the manufacturer's instructions to use the fusible.

figure 16

2 Turn the garment inside out and bring the edges of the cut together. Pin in place. Use a backstitch to sew the tear together in as narrow as seam as you can muster (figure 17). After you've finished, press the little seam to one side.

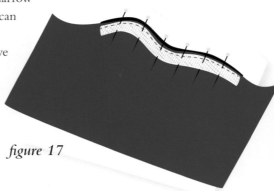

figure 17

Patching a Hole

Here's another for-instance. A buddy, whilst careless with his stogy, left a burn in your favorite tweed jacket. Right in the front, of course. This repair must be close to invisible, and thus (be warned) it may require a great leap of faith, depending on your level of trust in us, your loyal authors. Here goes:

1 Get some sharp little scissors and trim away (yes, that's right) the burned edges, taking as little fabric as you can (figure 18).

figure 18

2 Now, search around the inside of your jacket, and you're bound to find an inconspicuous spot from which to

figure 19

trim away enough fabric to cover the little hole on the outside of your jacket—the hem or the facing, for example, where the fabric is doubled on itself. Being careful to cut only the inside layer, snip away a circle of fabric that's a wee bit larger than your burn hole (figure 19).

3 Turn the jacket inside out and place it wrong side up on the ironing board. Cut a circle of paper-backed fusible web that's a little bit larger than your hole. Remove the paper backing. Follow the manufacturer's instructions to set the iron temperature for fusing. With the adhesive side down, put the circle of fusible over the hole, centering it just so. Fuse around

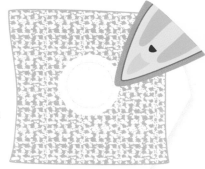

figure 20

the edges *only*, using just the tip of the iron (figure 20), being careful not to fuse the center of the hole to your ironing board!

(4) Flip the jacket and place it right side up. Take your little fabric patch and center it over the hole and fuse it in place (figure 21). To cover the hole you made on the inside of the jacket, use a commercial iron-on patch in a matching color.

figure 21

Remember—it won't be visible. Be sure to patch this helpful hole, though, or the fabric will ravel.

30-SECOND FIX

You're dashing to work to avoid being late for the third day in a row. You fly into your cubicle, toss your lunch into the secret hiding place in the cabinet of your desk, and promptly snag your elbow on the protruding screw in the hinge. You've got a rip in your sleeve! Find that private fixing place and remove your shirt. Once again, tape comes to the rescue. Turn the shirt inside out, place the torn edges together, and put a strip of tape across the tear. Remove the tape very carefully when you're ready to repair the tear for good.

EXIT STRATEGY

Spill coffee down your shirt before the big brunch/lunch/meeting/date with the [insert extremely important person in your life]*? We do hope your cell is charged. You're phoning in; you've suddenly developed a bad case of* [insert worst disease you can think of].

WHEN Calamity VISITS YOUR HOME

No refuge is safe. Disaster can strike at a moment's notice. Use your training to resolve any crisis, whether caused by man, woman, child, or beloved pet.

Repairing Bed Linens

Of course, a torn sheet isn't a real emergency. But if the tear is in the only set of sheets you've ever splurged on, and the thread count is through the roof, well yes it is an emergency. You've injured your wallet!

Bed linens commonly become torn or frayed in a couple of places—along the hemmed edges of flat sheets, and along the elasticized corners of the fitted sheets. When you notice a tear, be sure to repair it *before* you launder your linens or it will become worse after a trip through the washer and dryer. Here are some ways to rescue your linens from the rag bag.

If you have a tear along the hemmed edge (figure 1):

1 Bring the right sides of the sheet together along the tear. Pin.

2 Use a whipstitch (page 24) or the backstitch (page 23) to confront the calamity, beginning and ending the stitching about ½ inch (1.3cm) past the end of the tear. We'd recommend using the backstitch for extra security (figure 2). Stitch as close to the tear as you can.

figure 1

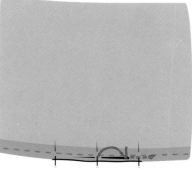

figure 2

Don't be tempted to use a commercial iron-on patch on your sheets if the tear you're patching will fall against your body. It will not be comfortable in the least. You'll have to count sheep all night long.

The corners of fitted sheets are constructed in a couple of different ways. High-quality sheets usually have a casing that covers the elastic, so you can't actually see it. Occasionally, the stitching in the casing comes loose and the elastic pops out (figure 3). Budget sheets are likely to have a visible band of elastic sewn around the corners; often, the sheet will pull loose from the elastic band (figure 4).

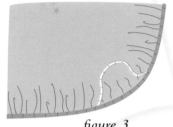

figure 3

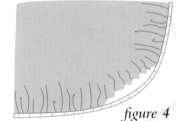

figure 4

If you've got a fancy sheet:

1 Don't even think about how much you paid for the set of sheets.

2 Pull the corner as taut as you can and tuck the elastic back inside the casing. Pin in place (figure 5).

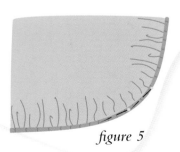

figure 5

3 Thread a needle with a double strand of thread. Stretch the corner taut as you repair the torn casing using the backstitch (page 23), as in figure 6.

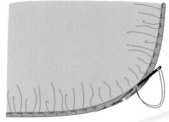

figure 6

If you've got a budget sheet:

1 Stare in dismay at the rip.

2 After a calming breath, turn the sheet inside out. Pull the ripped edge of the fabric over the elastic. Pin in place if you can (sometimes the elastic is very narrow).

3 Thread a needle with a double strand of thread. Stretch the corner taut and stitch the ripped edge to the elastic itself (figure 7), using the sturdy backstitch (page 23).

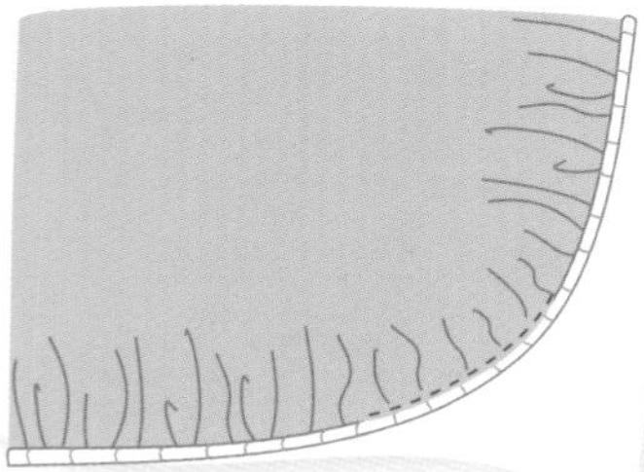

figure 7

Pillowcases can suffer from trauma, too. Typically, the opening edges of the cases become frayed. Here's a little trick to remedy this problem:

1 Turn the pillowcase inside out.

2 Turn up the frayed edge about ½ inch (2.3 cm). Pin in place (figure 8).

figure 8

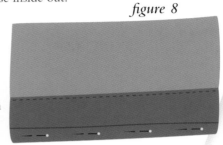

3 Use the hemstitch (page 25) to secure the folded edge. Now, you have a nice clean edge on your pillowcase.

You can have a little fun with this idea, too. Pin the edges up as in step 2 above, but use colorful embroidery floss to stitch the edge. A simple running stitch (page 23) will add a bit of welcome decoration to your repair (figure 9).

figure 9

Fixing a Tablecloth

Oh, my. You're planning your first party for your co-workers. Everything must be just so. Your decorating scheme revolves around your favorite tablecloth and matching napkins. When you pull the tablecloth out to iron it, you discover a forgotten gravy stain on said tablecloth. $&*$!!!

Remember when we talked about appliqué? Now is the time to brush up on that technique. A few well-placed appliqués will disguise that sneaky stain in no time. And you can exercise your creativity while confronting your crisis.

1 Choose a shape and cut out a piece of fabric that's large enough to cover the stain. (If you'd like, cut out several pieces to make a motif.) Cut a matching piece (or pieces) from paper-backed fusible web.

2 Following the manufacturer's instructions, apply the fusible web to the wrong side of the appliqué. Remove the paper backing and fuse the appliqué over the stain on the tablecloth (figure 10).

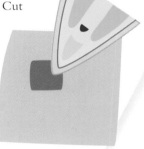

figure 10

3 Add a series of motifs if you're inspired (figure 11).

figure 11

There's an alternative way to add an appliqué, too, and this one is a bit more polished. We'll press under the raw edges of the appliqué before we apply it to the tablecloth. This is the method to use if your dinner party involves silver or flaming desserts.

1 Cut the appliqué(s) to size as described in step 1 on page 58, but add ½ inch (1.3 cm) of extra fabric all the way around (figure 12).

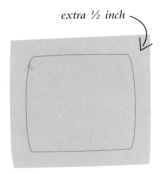

extra ½ inch

figure 12

2 Cut the fusible web to the size of the actual appliqué, (excluding the extra ½ inch [1.3 cm]), and adhere it to the back of the appliqué, following the manufacturer's instructions.

3 Now, remove the paper backing and (this is very important), press up the extra ½ inch (1.3 cm) around the edges, applying the iron to the edges *only* (figure 13). We do mean *only*. This step fuses the edges in place to create a finished look.

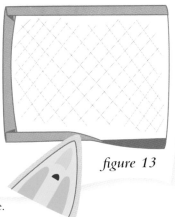

figure 13

4 Place the appliqué over the stain and fuse in place.

5 Use a running stitch (page 23) to sew all along the edge of the appliqué.

Indulge us for a moment as we share with you one more way to disguise stains and holes in a favorite tablecloth. Use ribbon or trim for real emergency decorating!

1 Measure the tablecloth and add 1 inch (2.5 cm) (figure 14). Cut the trim to this measurement.

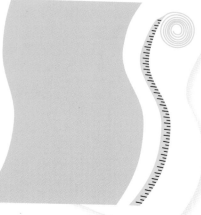

2 Fold ½ inch (1.3 cm) of the trim over to the wrong side of the tablecloth. Pin the trim along the tablecloth, covering the problem area. When you reach the end, fold the remaining end of the trim to the wrong side as you did at the beginning.

figure 14

3 Use the stitch of your choice to sew the trim to the tablecloth (figure 15).

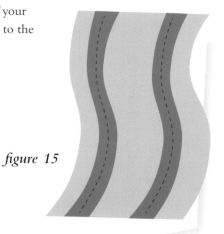

figure 15

Repairing a Worn Blanket

It is possible to freeze to death, of course, and surely we can all agree that this would constitute a true survival situation. If you have blankets in need of some reinforcement, we're here to help. Because blankets, comforters, and quilts are all pricey, it's in the best interest of your body temperature to counteract a little wear-and-tear.

A wool blanket usually has a binding covering the edges. Often, the binding experiences a crisis before the blanket itself does.

If you have an isolated tear in the binding:

1 Mend the tear with a whipstitch (page 24).

figure 16

2 Measure the width of binding, including both sides of the blanket (figure 16). Add 1 inch (2.5 cm).

3 Cut a piece of fabric to patch the mend. It should be the length that you measured in step 2, and wide enough to cover your stitching plus an extra ½ inch (1.3 cm).

4 Press under ¼ inch (6 mm) on each side of the patch.

5 Press under ½ inch (1.3 cm) on each end of the patch. Unfold one end and place the pressed fold to the edge of the binding. Stitch it in place using a backstitch (figure 17).

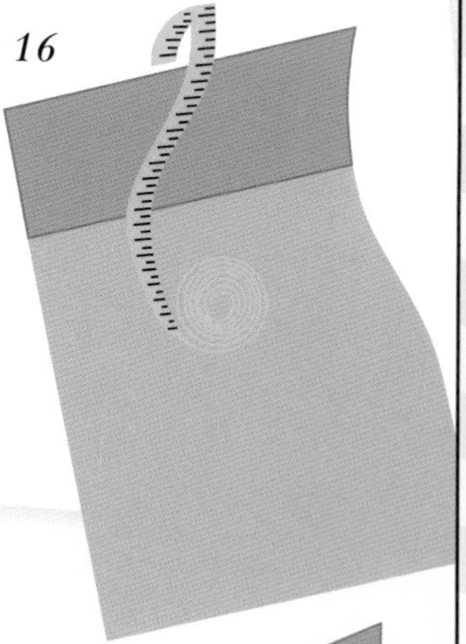

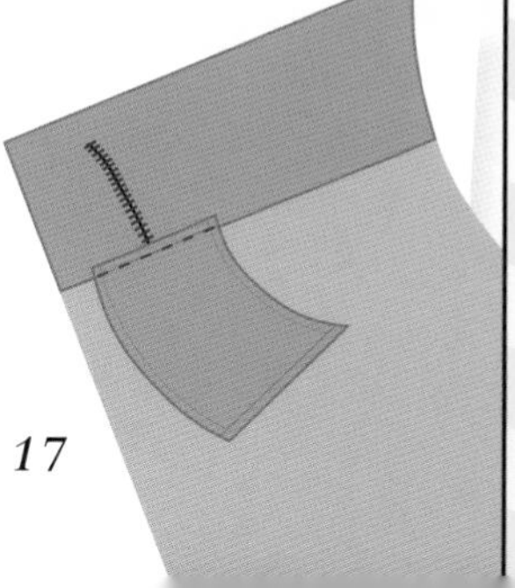

figure 17

6 Fold the patch over the binding to the other side. Stitch the folded end and the sides of the patch in place using a running stitch (page 23), stitching through all layers (figure 18).

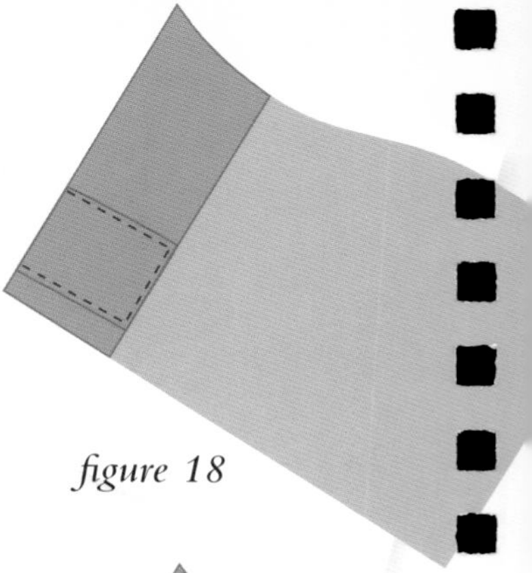

figure 18

The blanket can have its own problems. In particular, enemy moths may have used your blanket for an afternoon snack.

To patch a hole in a blanket:

1 Cut two identical patches that are large enough to cover your hole, adding an additional ½ inch (1.2 cm) all around.

2 Press under ½ inch (1.2 cm) on each edge.

3 Pin the patches in place, one on each side of the blanket (figure 19). Align them with one another as closely as possible.

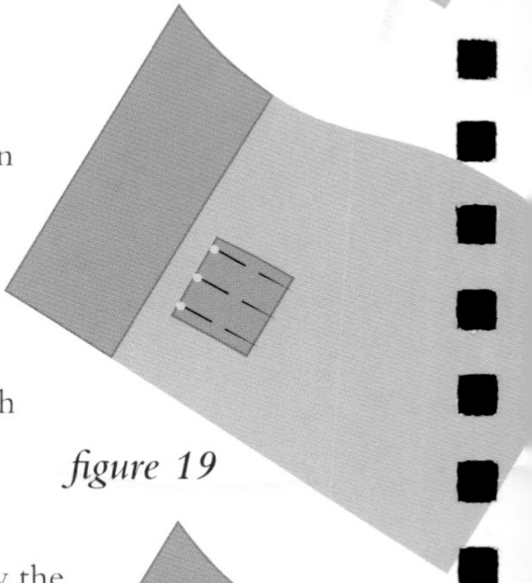

figure 19

4 Use a double strand of thread to sew the patches on, using a satin stitch (page 24). If you can, stitch through all layers, sewing on both patches at the same time (figure 20).

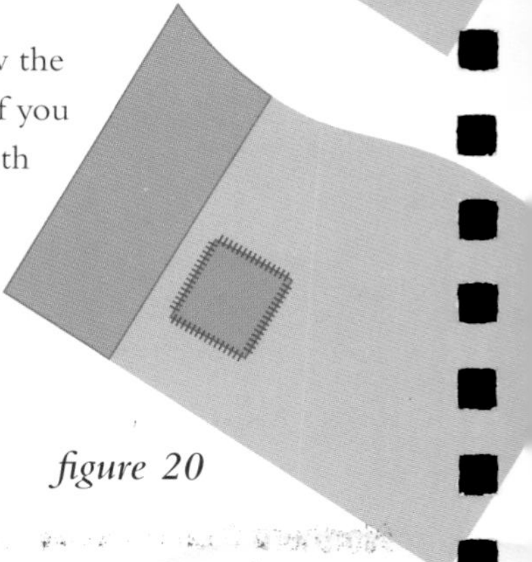

We suggest flannel for patching blankets. We'll talk more about buying fabric on page 107. It's an important sewing survival skill!

figure 20

Extending the Life of a Quilt

Dear Great-Aunt Mavis. In addition to giving you the fabulous lamp on page 73, she's also given you a quilt she made. It's actually quite lovely, but it's in desperate need of some reconstructive surgery.

We wouldn't dare suggest that you try to repair a true heirloom quilt (that's for a specialist), but an everyday quilt can be repaired by merely covering the worn patches with new patches.

1 Thank Great Aunt Mavis, despite the tear (figure 21).

2 Cut a patch from fabric that's the same size and shape of the worn patch, adding ¼ inch (6 mm) all around.

3 Press under ¼ (6 mm) inch on each edge.

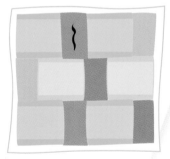

figure 21

4 Pin the new patch in place over the worn patch (figure 22).

5 Use a single strand of thread to slipstitch (page 25) the patch to the quilt, making the stitching as invisible as you can.

figure 22

Resuscitating Sofa Pillows

We unconditionally believe that dog is man *and* woman's best friend. But chewed-up shoes, torn-up furniture, gnawed books, soiled rugs...sheesh, when are you going to take that pooch to obedience school?

Pillows seem to be the favorite target of a bored pet. Case in point: you're about to host a dinner party for, say, your crusty new in-laws. Feeling ignored, Fifi gets busy in the living room while you're slaving away in the kitchen. Luckily, you *do* have the little kit we've thoughtfully supplied for you. Thread your trusty needle (doubled for strength), and read on.

If the pillow or cushion is coming apart along a seam:

1   Unzip the cover and pull out the insert. (No zipper? No problem! Skip to the next page.)

2   Turn the cover inside out and pin the offending edges together. The pillow may have piping; no problem. Just align the edges of the fabric and pin.

3   Whip the busted seam back together using the backstitch (page 23). Start sewing 1 inch (2.5 cm) away from the end of the still-sewn stitching. (The overlap strengthens that vulnerable spot.) Insert the needle to the right, and then back through ¼ inch (6 mm) to the left. Stick the needle back through at the end of the previous stitch, and repeat (figure 23).

figure 23

4   After you've repaired the tear, stitch an additional 1 inch (2.5 cm) into the still-sewn seam, and knot off. Turn the cover right side out, pop the insert back inside, and zip the pillow closed.

No zipper? Use the slipstitch to close up the seam from the exterior.

1   Slip the needle through one end of the open seam to anchor the thread (figure 24). Take a small stitch through the fold and pull the needle through.

2   Insert the needle directly opposite the end of the stitch you just made, and take a stitch through the other fold. Pull the edges to match snugly together. Try not to catch any of the fluff in your stitches.

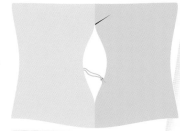

figure 24

3   Continue stitching (figure 25) until you reach the end of the hole, tie off, and snip.

figure 25

Your pillow's as good as new.
Fluff it, but before tossing it back on the sofa, threaten Fifi with death if she messes with it again.

Now, occasionally complications arise. Rather than
the seam coming open, let's say Fifi's pal Fido
has created a rip smack dab in the center of the
fabric. This Code Red calls for not only a repair,
but also for camouflaging tactics. If the fabric
of the pillow or cushion is torn:

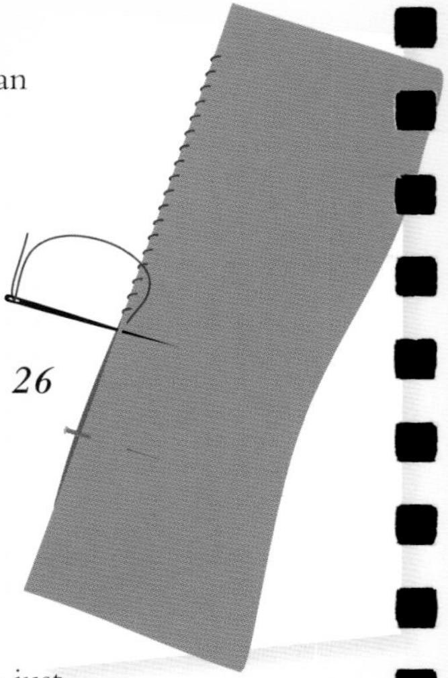

figure 26

1   First, address the repair. (Fido
can wait.) Open the zipper, remove
the insert, and turn the cover inside out.
Hold the rip closed with pins. Whipstitch
by inserting the needle perpendicular to
the fabric edge over and over again, creating
slanted stitches (figure 26). If there's no zipper, just
whipstitch the tear from the outside.

2   Decide how you want to disguise the problem area. A
commercial patch sewn or ironed over the scar? A floral-shaped
appliqué? A wide ribbon sewn across the entire pillow with
running stitch? Express your creativity—go for it! If you need
help with figuring out how to do the actual sewing for any of
these ideas, see Using Patches & Appliques on page 31, or consult
Adding Pizzazz When You Mend on page 34.

3   If you removed the insert in step 1, turn the cover right
side out again, replace its stuffing, and zip the pillow shut.

30-SECOND FIX

*Drape a throw blanket casually over the damaged cushion and pray
Fifi doesn't drag it off. Or chuck the pillow under the couch; with any
luck, Fido won't pull it out to flaunt his mangled prize in front of your
mother-in-law.*

Fixing Dog Beds

When they're not busy tearing things up, er, *playing*, exhausted doggies replenish their energy with refreshing naps. Considering that they have four sets of sharp claws per pooch, it doesn't take a crystal ball to figure out that a dog bed will need repairs at some point.

This is a perfect opportunity for a fun appliqué—wouldn't the outline of a big bone cut from white canvas look great? Or how about sewing on a few large circles cut out of terry cloth, with embroidered lines to resemble tennis balls? If you're feeling ambitious, you could even stitch lines so the balls appear to be "bouncing" across the bed.

1 Unless you relish the idea of looking and smelling like Chewbacca when you've finished sewing, remove the cushion and wash and dry the cover.

2 Turn the cover inside out. Hold the rip closed with pins, then whipstitch it using heavy upholstery thread. To do this, insert the needle perpendicular to the fabric edge, over and over and over again (figure 27). Knot and turn the cover right side out.

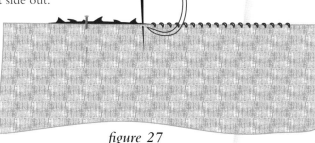

figure 27

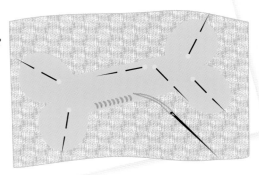

figure 28

3 Have you decided how to disguise the rip? If you want to make your own patch or appliqué, choose a strong fabric that will hold up to heavy use, and sew it on with a double strand of upholstery thread. Use a strong stitch such as satin stitch (page 24), which is a bunch of parallel stitches sewn closely to one other (figure 28).

4 Replace the cushion and zip it shut.

EXIT STRATEGY

Goodbye, pooch! Don't let the door hit you in the tail on the way out.

Hiding Threadbare Sofa Arms

You didn't think we were going to blame all damaged furnishings on dogs, did you? Oh, no, no…we're all too aware of the destruction cats can wreak. The artfully shredded carpeting. The tattered drapes. The easy chair that looks like a plucked chicken. One of us has even lived with a trio of cats that used the wall as a scratching post—*the wall!* And they had a scratching post, too.

So maybe you inherited an heirloom sofa and your little darlings have used the armrests to sharpen their claws. You could have the sofa reupholstered, but we bet you'd rather use the money to take a vacation to the Bahamas instead. (Uh-oh…what will the kitties do to the curtains while you're sunning on Nassau? We've got your back—turn the page.)

Instead of dropping a fortune on upholstering, just conceal the armrests under little slipcovers. The covers stay in place thanks to hook and loop tape, so the only thing you've got to sew are a few hems. When you buy the hook-and-loop tape, also purchase the special glue that adheres it to fabric.

1 Cut two squares of fabric, each oh, say 11 x 15 inches (27.9 x 38.1 cm). You probably won't be able to use fabric that matches the sofa, so find something you like. To hem each square, begin by turning each side under ½ inch (1.3 cm) and press (figure 29).

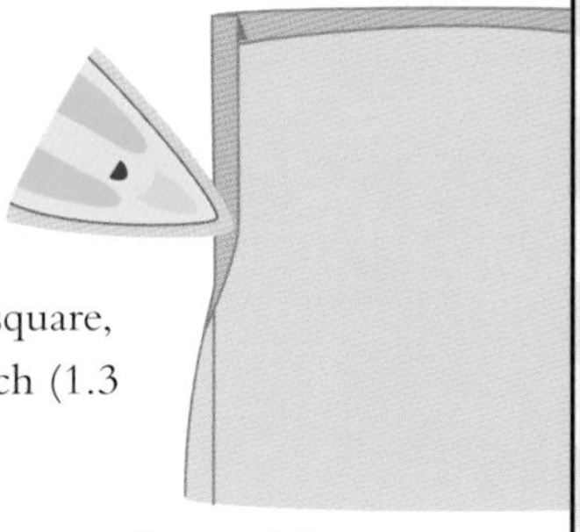

figure 29

2 Remember the way we repaired a hem with fusible web tape on page 43? You could use the same method to hem your slipcovers, if you'd like. Or, you could sew the hems with running stitch (page 23). Weave the needle in and out of the fabric, keeping the size of the stitches even and the stitching pretty close to the raw edge (figure 30).

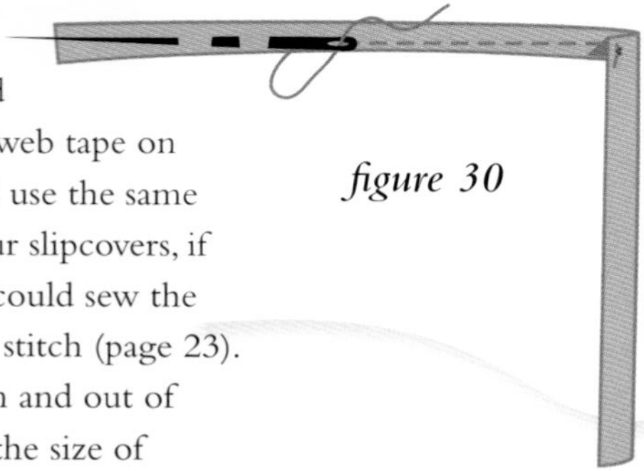

figure 30

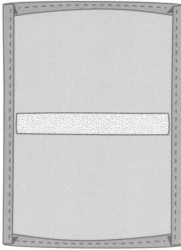

3 Follow the instructions with the hook and loop tape to glue one side of it to the middle of the armrest cover (figure 31), and attach the other half to the couch in the appropriate spot.

Don't forget the sunscreen.

figure 31

Mending Torn Curtains

Remember that vacation in the Bahamas mentioned on page 69? You did take it, right? So you return tanned and relaxed…and the feeling evaporates when you unlock the door. The cats went berserk with loneliness and used the sheers as a climbing wall!

Don't lose your cool. Use your advanced survival sewing skills to make creative repairs. Think of it as redecorating.

1 Address the repairs first. Hold tears closed with pins and whipstitch by inserting the needle perpendicular to the fabric edge over and over again, creating slanted stitches (figure 32).

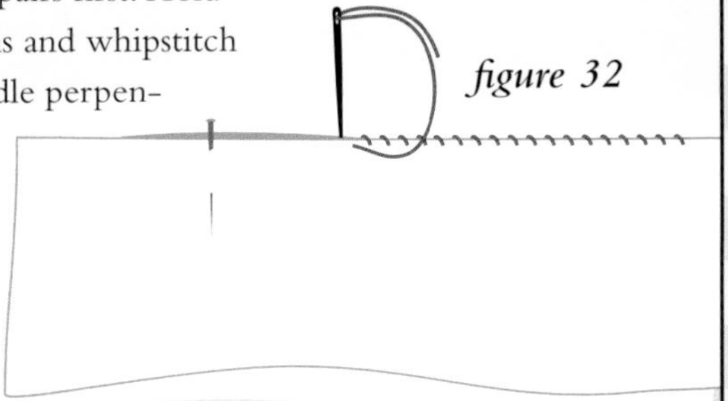

figure 32

2 How do you want to mask the problem area? You could sew on a floral-shaped appliqué; why, you could create an entire garden, if you wanted (figure 33). First cut out the floral shapes and pin them on top of the offending tears. Stitch them down with a simple running stitch around the edges. Then, add cute little centers in contrasting fabric.

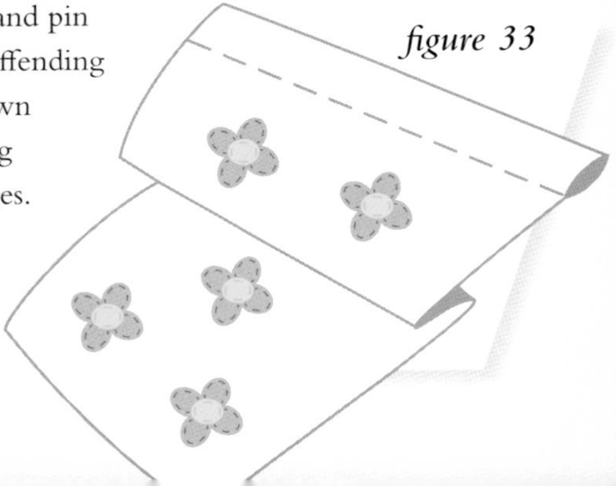

figure 33

3 If you prefer ribbon, how about pinning a few stripes down the length of the curtain and attaching them with running stitch (page 23), as in figure 34? Feel free to let your imagination run wild, but if you want help with figuring out the actual sewing for either of these, see Using Patches & Appliques on page 31, or consult Adding Pizzazz When You Mend on page 34.

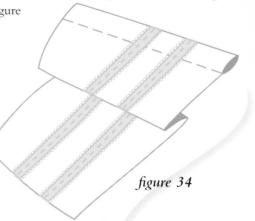

figure 34

And if you have a set of curtains and like to keep everything symmetrical, don't forget to trim both sides of the pair the same way.

EXIT STRATEGY

Got a friend who needs a pet?

Revamping Old Lampshades

Great-Aunt Mavis gave you this great old Victorian lamp that you've wanted ever since you were yea high, but her eyesight is pretty bad now, and she didn't notice that the fabric at the bottom of the shade is frayed. Have you priced new lampshades? After you recover from the shock, you'll be convinced to give the shade a facelift yourself. Let's shed some light on the matter, shall we? (Bonus: No sewing to do!)

1 Remove the shade from the lamp and carefully measure its circumference at the bottom, then add 6 inches (15.2 cm) as a fudge factor. You'll need to purchase this amount of trim.

2 Go shopping for fabric glue, clothespins, and some fabulous trimming. Bet you find so many—braid, gimp, pompoms, beaded fringe, looped gossamer organza rosettes, feather fringe, velvet trim, and rhinestone edging—that you have a hard time choosing!

3 Glue the trim to the bottom of the lampshade. Beginning at a seam in the shade and working your way around in sections, spread a thin layer of glue along the bottom of the shade and press the trim onto it. Keep the trim in place while it dries by using lots of clothespins (figure 35).

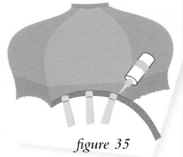

figure 35

4 After you're back at the starting point, cut the trim so it matches evenly with the end you first glued down and doesn't overlap. Let the glue dry completely before putting the shade back on the lamp.

WHEN MERELY
MERELY
Inconvenienced

Not all sewing mishaps are bona fide emergencies. In this chapter, we learn to repair annoying, but not life-threatening mishaps. A cool head and a quick needle will resolve most of these little problems.

Removing Pesky Labels

Isn't it annoying the way labels always seem to poke out of your shirt? And don't itchy tags drive you completely nuts?! While it's not a true emergency, you probably feel the urgent need to stop that scratchiness. So what's the best method for dealing with this?

If you don't mind a little sloppiness, the quickest method is to snip the label off on either side, near where it's stitched on (see figure 1). This prevents the label from sticking out of the shirt, but it unfortunately leaves behind the edges of the label that are still itchy. Washing can cause those edges to unravel and you'll end up with streamers of thread inside your garment. Instead, remove the label completely.

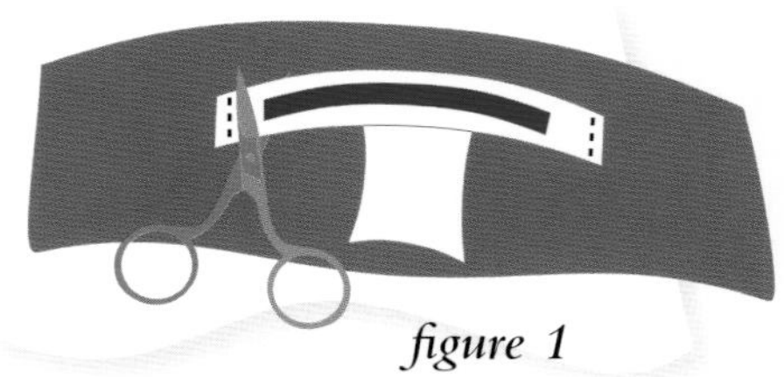

figure 1

1 Using a seam ripper, gently pick out the stitches on the left side of the label (figure 2).

2 Remove the stitches on the right side in the same manner. Done!

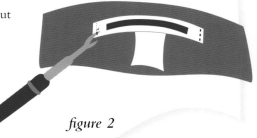

figure 2

Some manufacturers apparently want that label to stay in forever, so instead of tacking the label down on either end, they sew it into a seam. Removal will require a little more persistence on your part, but with your extensive training you're ready.

1 Working from the top, gently pick out as much of the seam holding the label as possible (figure 3). Remove only as much stitching as necessary.

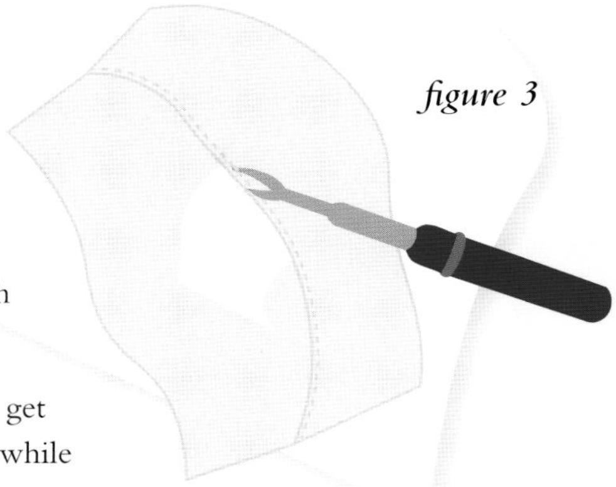

figure 3

2 Lift the label to get to the underside, and while gently tugging at the seam, carefully rip out any spots that didn't come loose in step 1 (figure 4).

3 After you've removed the label, sew the seam shut with tiny backstitches. Need a reminder of how to do that? See page 23.

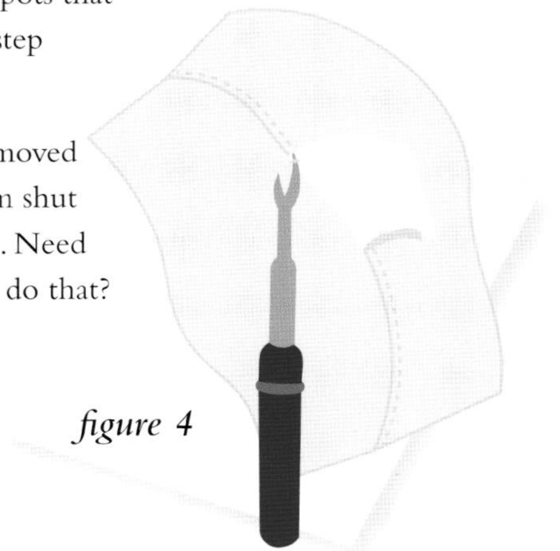

figure 4

Repairing Belt Loops

So one of the belt loops on your pants has gone on holiday. Chances are good your trousers will stay up and you don't have an emergency to avert. However, sewing the loop back down will keep you looking suave.

With your eagle eyes, you've probably noticed there's a hole in the pants (figure 5). Well, you can't very well stitch the belt loop to thin air, can you? So this is a two-part maneuver. First you patch the hole, and then you just make a few stitches to anchor the belt loop to the patch. The hardest part is figuring out what kind of cool fabric to use to cover up the hole.

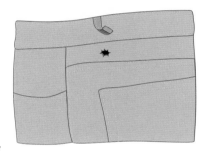

figure 5

1 Make the patch by cutting a small square of fabric. (A scrap 2 inches [5.1 cm] square ought to do the trick.) Turn under the edges ½ inch (1.3 cm) all around and press them. Pin the patch over the hole with both the pants and the patch facing right side up (figure 6).

figure 6

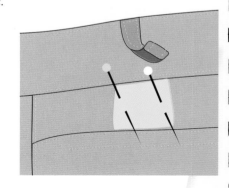

2 Using doubled thread in your needle, use the running stitch (page 23) to sew down the patch. Just weave the needle in and out of the fabric all around

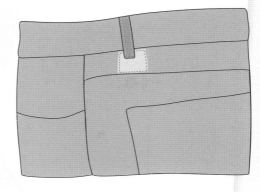

figure 7

the edge, keeping the stitches close to the edge and uniform in size. Then stitch the loose end of the belt loop to the patch with a few running stitches (figure 7). You could use a tack (page 26) to secure the belt loop, too.

Don't forget to remove the pins before wearing the pants. But you already knew that, didn't you?

30 SECOND FIX

Pull your shirt tail out. Actually, that's probably a 5-second fix!

Fixing Pockets

A hole in a pocket's no big deal, right? It's not like it shows. Except that cab ride home after you lose your car keys won't be cheap. And too bad you can't pay for it—because your money fell through the gap, too.

Okay, folks, thread your needle, go to your secret hiding place and turn the garment inside out.

1 In the area where the seam has come undone, match the edges of the pocket and pin them together.

2 Starting ½ inch (1.3 cm) to the right of the point where the seam came apart, begin stitching the fabric together using whipstitch. Remember that stitch? If not, see page 24.

3 Repeat, stitching toward the left (figure 8). Sew until you're ½ inch (1.2 cm) beyond the edge of the intact seam.

4 Tie a knot and snip off the excess thread.

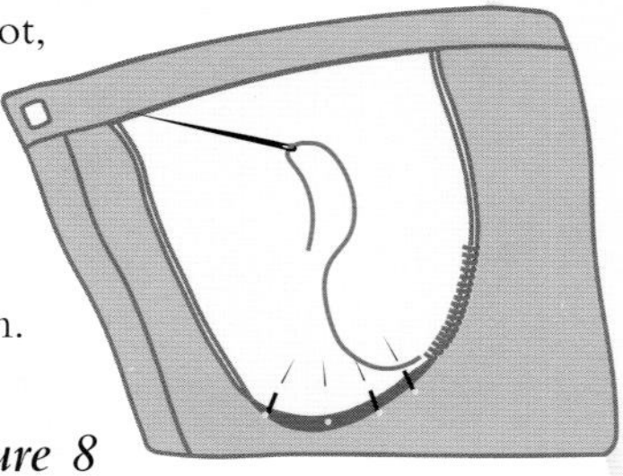

figure 8

figure 9

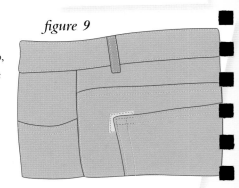

Sometimes your favorite jeans develop a hole where the pocket is stitched on to the pant. Darn it. No, silly—repair it. Remember how we fixed the belt loop on page 78? It's exactly the same idea. Put a patch over the hole and stitch the pocket to the patch (figure 9).

Putting Snaps in Gaps
+ Assorted Closure Dilemmas

You know those embarrassing gaps you sometimes get in the button plackets of shirts? This scenario can warrant emergency action, depending on who (your boss?) happens to notice that your shirt no longer covers you up. Fixing the problem is a snap—literally.

Snaps

Stitching a snap on the area that gapes will keep the placket closed. Use a small snap, so it won't be conspicuous. You'll notice snaps come apart into two different halves: one has a socket, the other, a ball. Here's how to sew each part on.

1 The socket part of the snap usually goes on the part of the garment hidden underneath the overlap. Hold the snap about ⅛ inch (3 mm) from the edge. Make a few tacking stitches (page 26) through one hole. Pass the needle between the fabric and the socket to the next hole, then make a few more tacking stitches there. Repeat until the socket's stitched down.

2 Sew the ball part of the snap to the underside of the garment's overlap, picking up just two or three threads of fabric so the stitches won't show on the right side. Use the same method to tack it down as you did with the socket side (figure 10).

figure 10

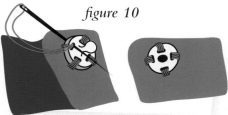

Now, to deal with that spot of the shirt that's yawning open, eyeball the midpoint between the two buttonholes, mark it with a pin, and sew on the socket side of the snap. Mark the position of the ball by buttoning the shirt, stick a pin or needle up through the hole in the socket, and center the ball part of the snap in that spot. Stitch in place (figure 11).

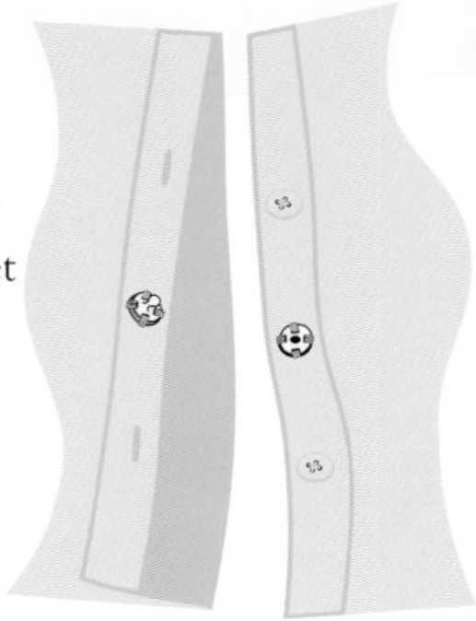

Replacing Hooks & Eyes

figure 11

Hooks come with either straight eyes or loop eyes; for edges that meet, use a loop eye, and for edges that overlap, use a straight eye. Stitch either type on with tacking stitches (page 26), starting with the hook; then mark the placement of the eye with a pin and sew it on. Pick up just a few threads of fabric so the stitches don't show on the right side of the clothing.

1 Use a few tacking stitches through each of the hook's holes to sew it to the inside of the garment, ⅛ inch (3 mm) from the edge.

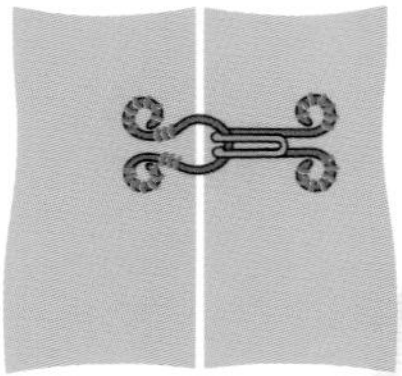

2 Tack a loop eye to the inside of the garment as shown in figure 12. To keep the eye flat, stitch it down along both sides of the loop. Tack a straight eye as shown in figure 13, also positioning the hook about ⅛ inch (3 mm) from the edge of the garment. Keep its hook flat by tacking it down under the curve of the hook.

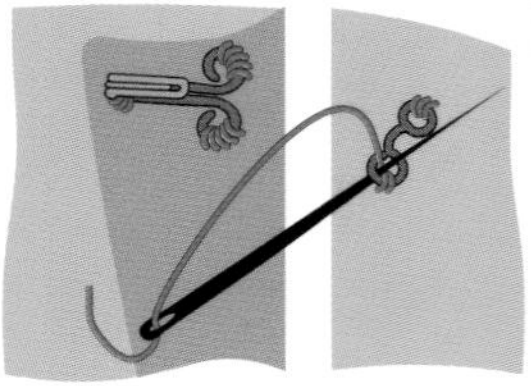

figure 12

figure 13

Reviving Frayed Buttonholes

The messy appearance of fraying buttonholes doesn't seem like a problem, but be advised that there could be an emergency brewing! The buttons can pop open without warning, leaving you feeling, uh, a little breezy. Avoid the unwanted exposure by fixing those buttonholes the way a pro would.

Use thread that matches the original buttonhole thread.

1 With a seam ripper, remove all the threads from the frayed buttonhole. Follow the outline of the original stitching when you rework the buttonhole.

2 Hold the garment right-side up, with the buttonhole horizontal. Begin sewing at the inside top edge of the buttonhole, poking your needle up from the wrong side of the fabric of the fabric.

3 Slide your needle back down through the buttonhole slit and stick it through from the wrong side of the fabric, just to the right of the first stitch; don't pull it all the way through, but stop when the tip of the needle protrudes ½ inch (1.3 cm) through the fabric, as shown in figure 14.

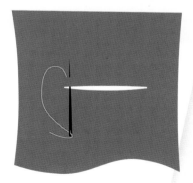

figure 14

4 Loop the thread counterclockwise around the needle with your fingers, first under the eye, then around the point. Repeat across (figure 15). As you pull the needle through, the looping creates a knot that rests along the edge of the buttonhole slit (figure 16).

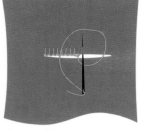

figure 15

5 Repeat steps 3 and 4, working around the buttonhole clockwise. Keep the stitches close together so that no fabric shows between the knots. At either end of the buttonhole, continue creating the same knots as you work your way around (figure 17).

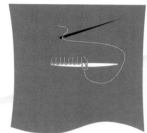

figure 16

6 After you make your way back to the original stitch, sew through the first knot, then tie off.

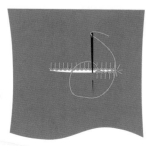

figure 17

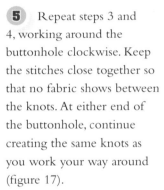

Altering Hems

Ah, the vagaries of fashion…short one season, long the next. It creates a crisis in your closet, because that long skirt that was so *in* last year makes you look hopelessly out-of-date now that minis are hot. But you don't have to keep spending to stay stylish. Just alter your hemlines.

Pull out your ironing board and plug in your iron: you'll need it to get a crisp hemline.

Shortening a hem

1 Figure out exactly how far up from the bottom you want the new hemline.

2 Using the measurement from step 1, mark the new hemline with pins placed parallel to the bottom (figure 18). Do this all around the garment.

figure 18

3 Turn the item of clothing inside out. Turn the fabric under along the pinned line, and insert pins perpendicular to it through both thicknesses of the garment (figure 19). Press along the new hemline-to-be, removing the first set of pins as you do so.

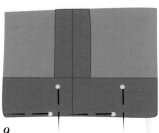

figure 19

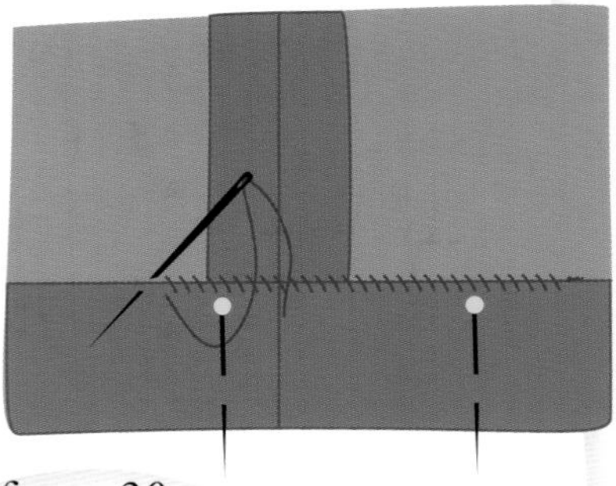

4 Thread your needle. To hemstitch around the garment, just pick up a thread or two of the garment,

figure 20

then insert the needle into the fold again (figure 20). Repeat until you've stitched around the entire hemline, then tie off.

Lengthening a hem

1 Carefully take out the current hem with a seam ripper. If the manufacturer used a straight stitch, just cut every few stitches (figure 21), then gently pull out the seam.

On the other hand, the manufacturer may have serged the garment, then hemmed it with commercial blindstitching. Serging is the "lacy" stitching on the edge of the fabric; don't rip that out because it prevents

figure 21

the fabric from raveling. The blindstitching looks kinda criss-crossed when you pull the hem up, as shown in figure 22. Take out the hem by ripping away the criss-crossed stitches (figure 23).

figure 22

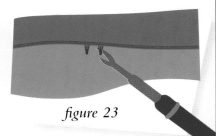

figure 23

2 Press away the original fold of the hem. (If the crease line is stubborn, mix equal parts white vinegar and water; apply this solution to a hidden part of the garment to make sure it's colorfast. If it is, apply it to the crease with a small brush, then try pressing again.)

3 Determine how far up from the bottom of the fabric you want the new hemline. Mark that measurement all around the garment with pins. Turn the garment inside out. Turn the fabric under along the pinned line, inserting pins perpendicular to it through both thicknesses of fabric as in step 3 on page 85. Press this hemline, removing the first set of pins as you do.

4 Thread your needle, and start hemstitching as described on page 25. Repeat until your fashion crisis has been resolved.

Guess what? These very principles also apply to the lengthening or shortening of sleeves and pant hems, too.

Resuscitating Lingerie

Fellas, go get an espresso. The ladies have a delicate crisis to discuss. Come back at the middle of the next page.

Because intimate garments are often flimsy, various problems can occur. Here's a good one to begin with: wayward straps. Free-spirited straps happen frequently on camisoles and nighties.

To repair a strap:

1 Pin the strap back in place, being careful that it's not twisted.

figure 24

2 With a double strand of thread, make a series of tacking stitches (page 26) on the wrong side of the garment (figure 24).

Sometimes we're bad girls and we forget to wash our dainties by hand. The washing machine is the enemy here, as bra hooks can become hopelessly mangled in the wringer. Fortunately, you can buy replacement hooks at your friendly fabric shop.

To replace a bra hook:

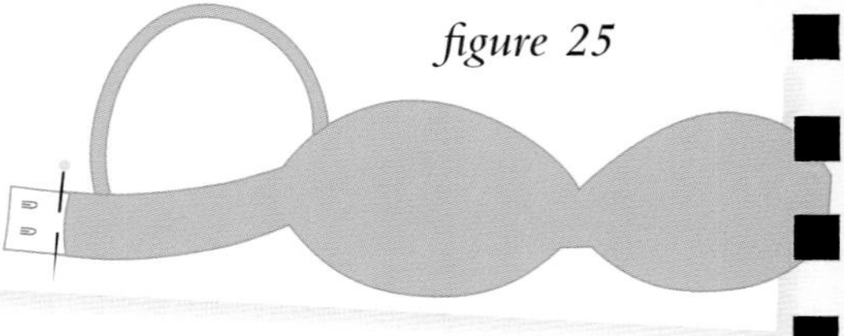

figure 25

1 Measure the length of the replacement piece. Subtract ½ inch (1.3 cm).

2 Trim away the end with the gnarled hooks to the measurement from step 1.

3 Place the replacement piece on the bra, overlapping the end by ½ inch (1.3 cm). Pin (figure 25).

4 Stitch the replacement piece to the bra with a tight whipstitch (page 24) or a tidy backstitch (page 23).

Okay, fellas, down the coffee. This one's for you, too. Occasionally, our knit undies become separated from the elastic, or the seams come loose. If you'll consult some of the previous pages in your manual, you can probably deduce how we're going to fix these things, because we've already talked about similar repairs in some of the early chapters.

1 If the fabric pulls loose from the elastic, use the technique for fixing sheets on page 56. It will look like figure 26.

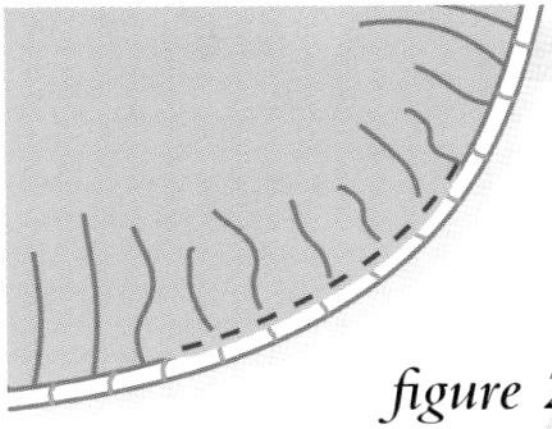

2 If the side seam has come undone, use the technique for repairing a seam on page 38. It will look like figure 27.

figure 26

figure 27

Repairing Linings

Linings exist to hide all the seams inside a garment and make it tidy on the inside. When linings in garments come apart, look on the bright side: you don't have to rush to fix them…unless it's a hem in a lining, which presents more of an immediate challenge.

If a seam in a lining comes apart, such as the center of the back, use the slipstitch to sew the two halves back together.

1 After threading the needle, insert it from the underside into the fold of the lining (figure 28). Pull the needle through to anchor the thread.

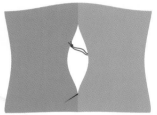

figure 28

2 Put the needle in directly opposite the stitch you just made, and take a stitch through the garment. Pull the edges so they match snugly together. Repeat, moving toward the opposite side of the split (figure 29).

figure 29

3 Tie off, and snip the thread (figure 30). Poke the knot inside the seam if you can.

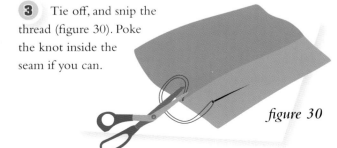

figure 30

Use the blindstitch (page 26), on the other hand, to hold down linings that have merely come loose from the garment, such as at the end of a sleeve or at the hem of a coat. The blindstitch allows the lining to have some movement inside the garment.

1 Iron the fold of the lining and place it against the garment; the lining will be shorter than the garment. You can pin them together if you need to.

2 Working with the lining facing up and holding the needle pointing left, pick up just a thread from the underside of the fold of the lining to anchor the thread and hide the knot (figure 31). As you stitch, hold the lining back with your thumb so you can get at the parts you need to and see what you're doing.

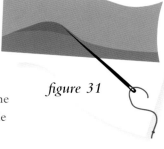

figure 31

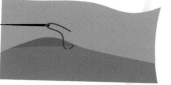

figure 32

3 Approximately ¼ inch (6 mm) to the left, but *in the garment*, take a small stitch with the needle still pointing left (figure 32). Pull the thread, but not completely tight.

4 Continue stitching, alternating between the lining and the garment (figure 33). Tie off.

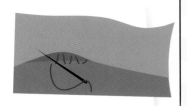

figure 33

Replacing Elastic

Droopy elastic can make a person feel so…insecure. But you don't have to trash a garment just because the waistband's gone south (or to your knees, as it were—now *there's* an emergency for you). Simply replace the elastic. Get 1 yard (.9 m) of elastic that's at least ⅛ inch (3 mm) narrower than the casing holding the original, worn-out stuff. (Shopping tips on page 106, remember.)

1 Near the back seam or a side seam, use a seam ripper to open the seam about 2 inches (5.1 cm) at the bottom of the casing (below the elastic). This will expose the elastic inside it (figure 34). Carefully cut the elastic and pull it out of the casing. Goodbye!

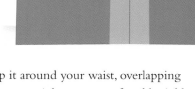

figure 34

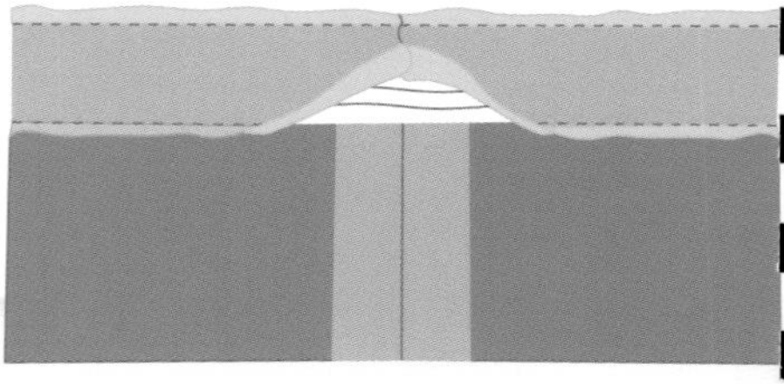

2 To figure out how much new elastic to use, wrap it around your waist, overlapping the end. It should feel snug, but not tight or uncomfortable. Add an inch (2.5 cm) to that measurement, and snip the elastic.

3 Anchor a safety pin in one end of the elastic and insert it into the opening you made in the casing (figure 35).

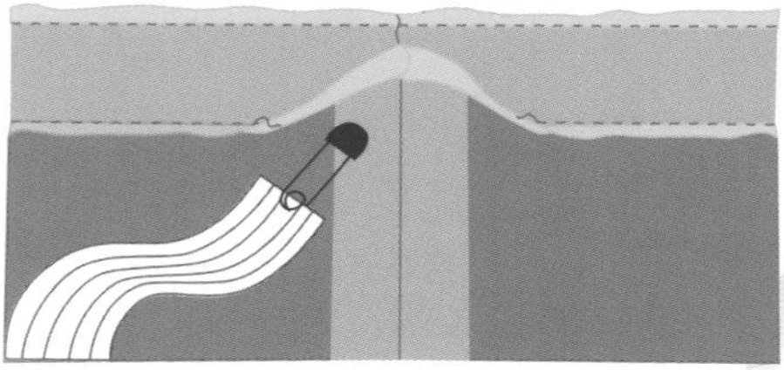

figure 35

4 Use your fingers to slide the safety pin along through the casing, pulling the elastic with it. Once you're halfway around, pin the loose, visible end of the elastic near the opening to avoid losing it inside. That would constitute a crisis!

5 After threading the elastic completely through the casing, remove both safety pins. Pull the ends of the elastic out of the casing a bit to make it easier to access them, then overlap them an inch (2.5 cm) and pin them to each other (figure 36).

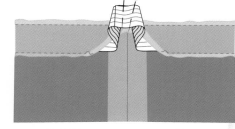

figure 36

6 Stitch them together, using backstitch (page 23) with a double thickness of thread, making a few rows of parallel stitching, as shown in figure 37.

figure 37

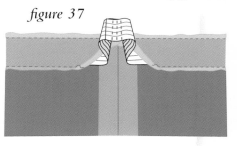

7 Hold the waistband at either side and stretch it open a couple of times to pull the elastic inside evenly. Pin the opening on the casing shut and use backstitch with a single thickness of thread to sew it closed.

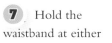

Fixing Handbags

Some people may not consider bags suitable material for a manual on survival sewing—but we know better. When your favorite bag goes kaput, it's a crisis of epic proportions.

Repairing Straps

If the stitching holding a strap to a metal ring has worn out, you can fix that easily. If the bag is leather, you should be able to make the repair through the existing holes.

1 Replace the strap through the ring (figure 38). Make sure not to add a twist in the process!

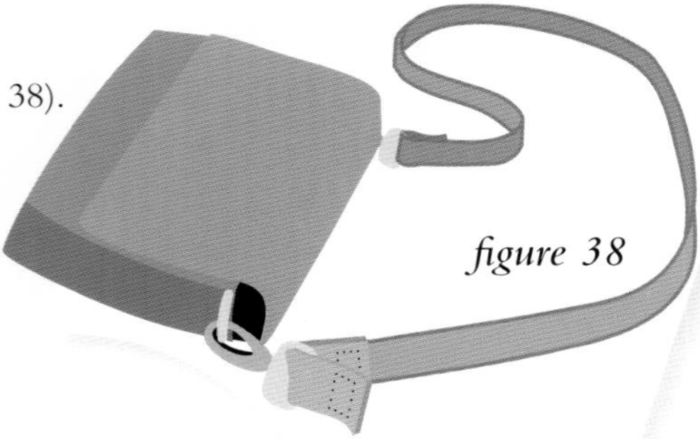

figure 38

2 Thread a needle with upholstery thread, double it, and make a knot. Anchor the needle through one layer of the strap only, inserting it from the wrong side. You should finish this step with the needle and thread facing outward (figure 39).

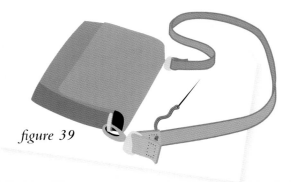

figure 39

3 Working from the outside, poke the needle through a stitching hole in one layer and also through the matching hole in the other layer (figure 40). Pull the layers of strap tightly together.

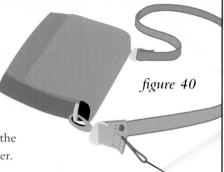

figure 40

4 Repeat in the adjacent hole. Continue sewing around the original stitching lines as described in step 3. When you reach the starting point, go through the first two stitches a few times and make a knot.

Mending Holes in Linings

When a seam opens in the lining of your bag, it's not really a big deal in the grand scheme of things, because it doesn't show, right? Except it does get a bit tiresome to keep hunting for the change and the keys and the gum that fall through it. Get ready to slipstitch (page 25).

1 Pull the lining as far out of the bag as possible. Thread the needle and make a knot.

2 Anchor the thread in one end of the open seam. Take a small stitch through the fold, then insert the needle directly opposite the end of the stitch you just made and take a stitch through that fold. Pull the edges together and keep stitching (figure 41) until the calamity has been alleviated. Tie off when done.

figure 41

Performing CPR on Garments

Sometimes emergency measures are required to save a favorite garment from the recycling bag. For instance: the weather's getting nippy, you pull out a cozy sweater that hasn't seen wear since last March, snuggle into it—and discover a moth hole. Darn...As a matter of fact, that's exactly what you're going to do to repair the hole.

Darn It!

The lost art of darning may sound mysterious, but it simply consists of sewing crossing lines of running stitches closely together to create a tight weave. The closer the color, texture, and thickness of the "thread" you select to the yarn originally used to make the sweater, the less the darning will show. Use a needle with a hole large enough to thread with a few strands of embroidery floss or yarn. Knotting the end of the thread's not necessary.

Before you begin, center the hole over a light bulb or a drinking glass. This allows the needle to glide over a smooth, hard surface, which will speed up your stitching.

1 Sew a perimeter of running stitches all around the hole, about ¾ inch (1.9 cm) from its edge. Do this by bringing the needle up through the fabric, then down, then up again (figure 42).

figure 42

2 On one side of the hole, make a few teeny running stitches in the intact part of the sweater. Sew vertically, starting and ending beyond the hole's edges. To avoid changing the shape of the garment, don't stitch tightly. Make another row of stitches parallel to the first, a little closer to the hole.

3 Keep making parallel rows of stitching, placing each closer to the hole than the last. When you reach the hole, take the thread or yarn over the hole and into the fabric on the other side to form a sort of bridge over the hole (figure 43). Keep working in this manner until you have a square of parallel rows of running stitches.

figure 43

4 Make a set of stitches perpendicular to the first ones (figure 44), working in the manner described above, but weave the thread in and out of the first set of stitches when you reach the hole itself.

Secure the excess thread by running it back and forth a few times through the knitted fabric of the sweater then trimming it, but don't make a knot.

figure 44

Frayed Not

One of us has a coat that she's adored for years—but unfortunately, all that lovin' is starting to show. One front edge looks tired and worn, but you don't think that coat will go to a thrift store anytime soon, do you? That's what fabulous trims are for!

Wouldn't striped grosgrain ribbon look fabulous edging the front of a coat? You can even do this if your coat doesn't look shabby, of course.

1 Measure the front edge of the coat. Add 6 inches (15.2 cm) to be safe, and get that length of 2-inch (5.1 cm) ribbon.

2 Work on the inside of the coat, on the outer part of the overlap. Turn one end of the ribbon under ½ inch (1.3 cm). With the turned-under part facing down, match the edge of the fold to the top of the coat's neckline. The ribbon should overlap the coat by ½ inch (1.3 cm), with 1½ inches (3.8 cm) floating free— that's the part that will eventually show on the front (figure 45). Pin the ribbon all along the edge of the coat, turning the bottom under ½ inch (1.3 cm) in the same way you did at the neckline.

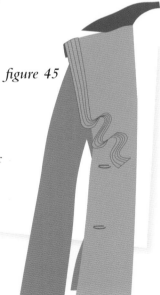

figure 45

3 Stitch the ribbon down using backstitch. To do that, after anchoring the thread at the right-hand edge of the top end of the ribbon, insert the needle to the right, and then back through ¼ inch (6 mm) to the left. Stick the needle back through at the end of the previous stitch. Repeat again and again, stitching to the other end of the ribbon (figure 46). Remove the pins.

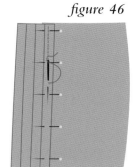

figure 46

4 Flip the coat so that the front is facing you. Fold the ribbon over to the front and pin it in place (figure 47). Backstitch along its left edge.

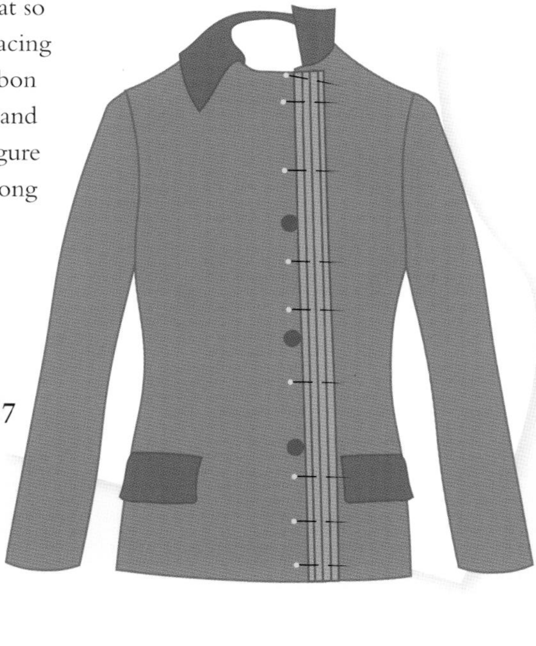

figure 47

You could do something similar to the ends of the sleeves—or, instead, you could go totally glam by covering them in fake fur. (At this point, you're a fully qualified sewing survivalist and you know what's best.) Here's how to camouflage ratty-looking cuffs.

1   Measure around the sleeve near the edge. Add 1 inch (2.5 cm) to that measurement, and jot that number down. Next, decide how wide to make the cuff (3 inches [7.6 cm] is probably good for a coat) and add 2 inches (5.1 cm) to that measurement. Draw a rectangle on some scrap paper, with the sides being the length of each of these measurements (figure 48). This is your pattern piece for the fake fur.

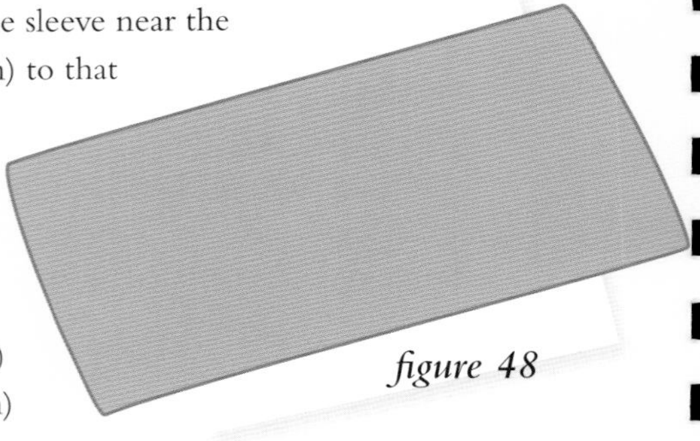

figure 48

2   Cut out the pattern piece, and pin it to some fake fur. Cut it out, and repeat to make another cuff.

3   Fold each rectangle of fake fur in half widthwise, with the fuzzy part facing in; match the two short edges and pin them together. Backstitch along the edge of each, ½ inch (1.3 cm) away from it (figure 49). Need a refresher on backstitching? See page 23.

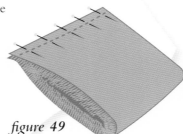

figure 49

4 Okay, so now you should have two fake-fur tubes. Turn each right side out, and slide one over each sleeve, matching the seams. Each fake-fur tube should extend 1 inch (2.5 cm) past the edge of the garment. Pin each tube to the sleeve to keep it in place (figure 50), then turn the sleeves inside out. Watch the pins!

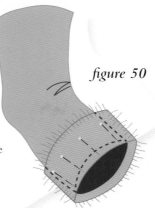

figure 50

5 Remember that 1-inch (2.5 cm) extension? Fold it over the edge of the sleeve, pin it flat, then stitch it down using hemstitch (page 25). Here's how: anchor the needle in the garment, then insert it into the fake fur slightly to the left and working from below. Pull the thread through, then insert the needle into the garment slightly to the left of the previous stitch. Repeat, alternating needle insertion into the fur and the garment (figure 51). Continue all the way 'round, and do the same to the other sleeve.

figure 51

6 Turn the sleeves right side out again. Turn under 1 inch (2.5 cm) on the free edge of the fake fur, pin it, and use hemstitching to keep it in place. Make the stitches tiny so they don't show.

NOT YOUR, Grandma's SEWING BASKET

After all this training, it's time to test the hardware that will allow you to make emergency repairs in the field. There's no flowery needlepoint basket here—this is survival gear, neatly tucked away into the convenient pouch in the back of the book.

What's in the Kit

Full attention, please. Here are the tools that will allow you to survive embarrassment and disaster. For reference, flip to the pouch as needed. Remember this section when it's time to buy more supplies, so you can buy the size included here, if you like.

Needles

We've provided you with two needles. The first is a #7 sharp, which is for general garment repair. The second is a #9 milliner, which is better for repairs on heavier fabric, such as pillows and so on.

Thread

You've got three little spools of thread—use the white on light colors, the black on dark colors, and the gray on anything in between.

Buttons

We've generously supplied three buttons, each a different size and color. The little button (⅜"/9mm) is blouse size; the medium one (⁷⁄₁₆"/11mm) is shirt size; and the largest button (¾"/20mm) is just right for pants.

Snaps

Please find enclosed three sets of snaps—tiny (size 4/0), small (size 3/0), and not-so-small (size 2/0).

Hooks and Eyes

For your sewing survival, we've given you two different types of hook and eye closures, both in size 2, a standard size. If you remember your previous training, the straight eye is used on garment edges that overlap, while the loop eye is used on garment edges that meet.

Scissors

You have one pair of standard-issue mini scissors in your kit.

Straight Pins

We've provided you with a nice dozen straight pins. It's a good idea to keep them in The Official Survival Sewing Needle Base in your kit; if they're secured in said base, you won't be poking yourself with them while you're reaching inside for supplies.

Safety Pins

For those quick fixes, please utilize the two safety pins found within. One is a little size 00, the other a larger size 1.

Fusible Web Tape

To cope with emergencies, you'll find two yards (1.8 m) of fusible web tape in your survival pouch. If you've failed to retain how to use this product, see the No-Sew Fix on page 43.

Needle Threader

For the shaky of hand or the far of sight, see the needle threader.

Ruler/Bookmark

Here is a multitasking tool: a clever little ruler that also serves as a bookmark.

How to Restock Your Supplies

Well, it seems like an easy enough concept to walk into a fabric shop and buy more thread and needles and so on. But what if you've never been in a fabric shop before? Let's take a field trip: your authors will give you a guided tour of the facility.

Buying Notions

Needles, thread, pins, and so on are referred to as *notions*. Your fabric shop will most likely have the majority of these things hanging on the wall, organized by type of thing and/or color. Here's how to look for replacements for your kit.

Needles. For general purposes, look for sharps for garment repairs, or milliners for home dec fixes. (Needles have funny sizing; the smaller the needle, the larger the number.) Should you need any specialty needles (such as an embroidery needle) you can also find them in the same section.

Thread. Look for thread labeled "all-purpose." If you're having trouble matching a specific color, go a shade darker rather than a shade lighter. If you need heavy-duty thread for a home dec calamity, you'll probably find a special display of this type of thread.

Buttons. You'll see scads of buttons displayed on a wall. They're usually organized by color, then size. If you're buying a replacement button and don't know what size you need, measure the buttonhole and subtract ⅛ inch (3 mm).

Snaps. Snaps are usually offered in either black or nickel finishes, and in an array of sizes. Sometimes you can purchase a variety of snaps in one package.

Hooks and eyes. You'll probably find these closures hanging near the snaps. They too come in different finishes and sizes; the general size 2 will probably serve most of your needs.

Scissors. If you want to purchase a full-size pair of scissors that will still fit into your pouch, consider a pair of embroidery scissors or a small pair of sewing scissors. Fabric shops usually have a special display of scissors and have models that you can try on for size.

Straight pins. There are pins with colorful glass heads, colorful plastic heads, little flower heads…you name it. But for basic sewing, pick up a package of size 17 dressmaker pins. The pins will probably be in close proximity to the needles.

Fusible web tape. Look for this product on a roll, just like regular tape. It may be sold under a fancy name, so ask for help if you can't find it right away.

Needle threader. These are usually sold three to a package, and they'll be near the needles and pins.

Ruler/bookmark. No, you can't replace your Official Survival Sewing ruler at your fabric shop. But you can buy a tape measure.

Miscellaneous. Any other supplies we've mentioned (elastic and so on) can also be purchased at the fabric store.

Buying Fabric

Remember that we suggest making patches and appliqués out of purchased fabric? Well, here's how to buy it. Fabric is sold by the yard, or by the increment of a yard. Garment fabric (the kind usually needed in emergency sewing) is generally displayed on bolts; if you look on the end of the bolt, you'll normally find the price of the fabric per yard and its fiber content.

You'll have to buy a minimum amount of fabric, like ⅛ yard (11.4 cm). Sometimes fabric shops will sell remnants, or leftover yardage, for a song, so maybe you can find what you need in the bargain bin. Be advised that you'll most likely have to buy the entire remnant, but often you'll still save a bundle.

30 SECOND FIX

In case your sleuthing skills are lacking, don't neglect the most important resource at your disposal—the salespeople! Be sure to ask if you have any questions about notions or fabric. They're professionals.

Cool Stuff in the Fabric Store

You don't have to visit a fabric store while under duress, you know. There's some interesting stuff that can make your life a little easier and your clothes a little spiffier.

Replacement pockets. You can buy an entirely new pocket for your clothes. Who knew?

Repair pockets. You can also buy iron-on repair pockets. No sewing involved whatsoever. Who knew (redux)?

Fabric mending tape. If you just need to make just a tiny repair, check this stuff out. It's less bulky than a patch and simply irons on.

Replacement straps. In addition to adding new hooks to your lingerie, you can also purchase new straps.

Lint shaver. These remarkable gadgets clean up fuzz balls and lint from clothing and upholstery. It's a great tool to rejuvenate vintage sweaters and coats, as well as revive a piece of flea-market furniture.

Rug binding. The iron to the rescue again! To prolong the life of a rug, add this material all around the edges.

Industrial hook-and-loop tape. Did you know you can use this stuff to hang tools in your garage? No kidding.

Alternate Tools

The motto of one crack fighting force is *semper preparate*, which means "always prepared" in Latin. Although we hope to have equipped you to immediately respond to any sewing crisis, we know all about life's unpredictable little bombshells. Our solution: improvise!

Dental floss. Out of thread? Think like a medic and head to the medicine cabinet. In a jam, you can substitute dental floss, waxed or not. As an additional benefit, you'll smell minty fresh all day!

Tape. No needles or thread? If the skirmish is contained (just a wee bit of a hem coming undone, for example), and you only have time for a quick defensive maneuver, apply tape as a temporary solution.

Stapler. Got a situation that requires strategic action? Call in the big guns! If you're at work, whip out a stapler to tackle seams or bigger problems, if you dare.

Fabric glue stick. You can also keep sewing encounters permanently under control if you speak softly, but carry a fabric glue stick. Just follow the manufacturer's instructions.

Pins. Seam ripper gone AWOL? Call the MPs—the Metal Pins, that is. In a pinch, use safety pins, straight pins, or even needles to pull out seams.

Paper clip. Got a stubborn zipper that won't zip up because the pull's gone missing? Simply slide a paper clip through the hole in the zipper.

Fuhgeddaboutit

At this point, you've probably learned that your fearless field generals (otherwise known as your authors) can tackle just about any sewing emergency. However, there are emergencies, and then there are hopeless situations. The latter require the deployment of professional reinforcements.

In the Closet

Here are some circumstances that exceed the level of training provided in this book. The first scenarios involve your wardrobe.

Repairing a Zipper

Oh, we wish we could be more optimistic about surviving this trauma on your own. Zippers can be repaired or replaced, but it involves so much surgery (carefully removing this and carefully replacing that) that it's honestly best left to a professional.

LONG-TERM FIX: *Find a tailor or an alterations specialist.*

Altering the Fit of a Garment

Other than altering a hem, which your highly trained authors have taught you how to do, true alterations also involve the same type of surgery mentioned above. A nip here and a tuck there can be complicated maneuvers.

LONG-TERM FIX: *Find a tailor or an alterations specialist.*

Repairing an Expensive Sweater

When you invest in a yummy cashmere sweater, you generally get a little bit of extra yarn. This is your present for spending so much money! No, really, you're given this yarn in case a hole springs up in your sweater. Unless the hole is in a discreet location, you shouldn't try to darn it yourself.

LONG-TERM FIX: *Take your sweater and extra yarn to an alterations specialist.*

Fixing a Leather Garment

Now, leather is a different animal. We're speaking literally here. Sewing on leather requires some serious skill. Please, please, take your leather (or suede) jackets to a pro.

LONG-TERM FIX: *Look for an alterations professional who specializes in leather repair.*

Around the House

Sometimes household situations get beyond your control.

Neutralizing Pet Damage

If Kitty has really gone to town on your curtains, we offer up only one solution—get rid of the cat. Just joking, of course.

LONG-TERM FIX: *Invest in new curtains. Call a cat whisperer.*

Repairing a Rug

If Fido has decided your antique rug is a chew toy, we don't advise trying to reweave it yourself.

LONG-TERM FIX: *Look for a dry cleaner or rug merchant who specializes in repair. Send Fido to obedience school stat.*

Saving a Vintage Quilt

Great-Aunt Mavis's quilt doesn't really fall into this category. But if you have a family heirloom you'd like to preserve, there are folks who are specially trained in repairing quilts.

LONG-TERM FIX: *Search online for a quilt conservator.*

Acknowledgments

Our little sortie into *Survival Sewing* wouldn't have been possible without the contributions of many talented people. Art Director Kristi Pfeffer and Associate Art Director Shannon Yokeley have carefully crafted an artsy manual for the sewing-challenged population. What a fabulous little book! And J'aime Allene patiently developed all the helpful (and fun) illustrations that you see here. Thanks to these production professionals who brought this project to life.

And lastly, we must thank Great-Aunt Mavis, without whom this book couldn't have been written. Just kidding—there is no Great-Aunt Mavis! Nathalie made her up. But each of us had aunts and mothers and grandmothers who felt it was important that we learn to sew, and we thank them for that.

Nathalie & Valerie

Index